Ten Tea Parties

TEN TEA PARTIES

PARTIES

Patriotic Protests
That History Forgot

BY JOSEPH CUMMINS

QUIRK BOOKS
PHILADELPHIA

Library of Congress Cataloging in Publication Number: 2011933426

ISBN: 978-1-59474-560-7

Printed in the United States of America

Typeset in Bembo and Old Claude

Designed by Doogie Horner
Production management by John J. McGurk

Cover and interior illustrations courtesy the Bridgeman Art Library
On the cover: *The Boston Tea Party, 16th December 1773*. Engraving.
Private collection/The Bridgeman Art Library.

Quirk Books
215 Church Street
Philadelphia, PA 19106
quirkbooks.com

10 9 8 7 6 5 4 3 2 1

THE PEOPLE SHOULD
NEVER RISE, WITHOUT
DOING SOMETHING TO BE
REMEMBERED—SOMETHING
NOTABLE. AND STRIKING.
THIS DESTRUCTION OF THE
TEA IS SO BOLD, SO DARING,
SO FIRM, INTREPID AND

INFLEXIBLE, AND IT MUST
HAVE SO IMPORTANT
CONSEQUENCES, AND SO
LASTING, THAT I CAN'T
BUT CONSIDER IT AS
AN EPOCHA IN HISTORY.

—*From the diary of John Adams,*
December 17, 1773

Introduction

What discontents, what dire events,
From trifling things proceed?
A little Tea, thrown in the Sea
Has thousands caused to bleed.

—*Anonymous New Hampshire poet*

I t was more than just a *little* tea, of course. The tea that dozens of patriots dumped into Boston Harbor on the chilly evening of December 16, 1773, amounted to more than 92,000 pounds. Tall piles of the stuff floated like huge haystacks in the dim moonlight of the bay. And in the days that followed, many British observers wondered if the residents of Boston had gone insane.

After all, weren't these the same colonists who consumed between 1,200,000 and 2,000,000 pounds of tea a year? One-third of America's three million inhabitants drank tea twice a day. Yet now this hearty and warming stimulant was being tossed to the seagulls like so much wharf trash?

What happened *after* the Boston Tea Party was even more remarkable: Other colonists, men and women widely separated from Bostonians in culture and outlook, rallied behind their Massachusetts brethren. Up and down the eastern seaboard, from York, Maine, to Charleston, South Carolina, colonists dumped, burned, and boycotted tea. They threatened those who delivered its leaves—be they ships' captains or humble peddlers—with everything from tarring and feathering to financial ruin. They scorned neighbors who drank tea and concocted an entirely fictitious sickness narrative around the beverage; they claimed tea stunted growth, turned men into pygmies, and transformed women into, as one patriot writer put it, "God knows what." They claimed that tea was stomped into chests by Chinese men with dirty feet, that it was infested with bugs.

This book tells the largely forgotten stories of ten colonial-era tea parties—protests in which tea was boycotted, destroyed, or worse. In these tales, Americans banded together to wage an economic war. And make no mistake—despite the tea party's more theatrical and carnivalesque trappings, this was *war*, with clear threats of violence directed at all those who dared to disagree with the patriots. When tea merchant Anthony Stewart was forced to set his ship *Peggy Stewart* ablaze in Annapolis, the mob deliberately engineered the conflagration to occur in front of the house where his wife, Peggy (the ship's namesake), was giving birth to their child.

Tea parties were not pretty, but then neither was the revolution. Taken together, these ten examples form an untold narrative of American independence, a narrative that contains the DNA of future American protest movements. Over the course of the nation's history, when times are tough and the chips are down, Americans have put aside their geographical and cultural differences to band together as a nation, as one. That had never happened before these early tea parties. In them, colonists overcame what historian T. H. Breen calls "local jealousies and mutual ignorance, profound fear and clashing identities" to find "a common political vision"—what one tea-burning group of citizens called "a general American union."

These ten tea parties are among the most important and influential milestones in America's growth and development—and it's a shame that so many are largely forgotten. Whenever the nation faces a challenge—whenever times require us to cooperate and serve together—the tea parties serve as an illuminating and inspiring example of all that Americans acting together can achieve.

CHAPTER ONE

Tea and the Company

"[Great Britain] believe[s] that threepence on a pound of tea, of which one does not drink perhaps ten pounds a year, is sufficient to overcome the patriotism of an American."

Benjamin Franklin, in a letter to Thomas Cushing

S ee if this story sounds familiar: During a severe financial recession, the government of the world's most powerful country discovers that its largest corporation—let's call it Corporation X—is rife with corruption, mired in debt, and facing financial collapse.

And although the corporation's directors probably are guilty of criminal behavior, the government won't consider allowing the business to go down the tubes. It's simply "too big to fail." Its finances are intertwined with those of the government and various national institutions much like veins and arteries grip a beating human heart.

If you think the only solution is a massive corporate bailout, you're right—only the corporation in question is not Merrill Lynch circa 2008 but the East India Company in 1773. It's hard to overstate the incredible influence of the East India Company in the eighteenth century. Imagine a Microsoft or Google with governmental permission to mint money, acquire territory, maintain a standing army, enter into foreign wars, and make peace treaties, and you'll have some idea of its might.

The company was founded more than 170 years before the American Revolution. As the 1500s came to a close, England had defeated the Spanish Armada and established itself as a sea power to be reckoned with, but it struggled to break into the burgeoning trade with the East, a lucrative business that had been cornered by the Dutch and Portuguese. This situation ended abruptly when a frustrated Queen Elizabeth I chartered, on the last day of 1600, a consortium of English merchants known as the Honorable East India Company (EIC), to which she granted a monopoly on all British trade east of the Cape of Good Hope. Thus emboldened, the EIC went on to become the world's most powerful trading company, a position it held for the next 250 years.

Like any huge corporation, the East India Company had shareholders who expected hefty returns on their dividends, and for many decades the EIC did not disappoint. Its fleets of armed merchants carried gold, silver, silk, cotton, spices, and opium across the oceans. They elbowed the Portuguese and Dutch out of the way and took India by storm, setting up dozens of trading posts, making deals with local Mughal rulers who were willing to cooperate, and launching armed attacks against those who would not. By 1767, the EIC controlled much of the state of Bengal, in eastern India, essentially ruling a population of twenty million. Thousands of young eighteenth-century Britons journeyed to company outposts to make their fortunes. The opportunity offered equal amounts of risk and reward, as demonstrated by the so-called two-monsoon rule: if a Briton could survive two monsoons (or three years) without falling prey to one of India's fatal illnesses, he was likely to escape the subcontinent alive and wealthy. Never mind that the Indian people supplying goods and labor to the EIC were plummeting ever deeper into poverty.

As the eighteenth century progressed, the East India's business evolved, with increasing amounts of its wealth being derived from a single commodity. This product was easy to obtain and transport and didn't perish on long ocean voyages. Best of all, there was huge demand for it in both the old world and the new. That product, of course, was tea. The East India Company imported tons of tea into Great Britain, up to thirteen million pounds annually, after which it was sold by various middlemen. By the mid-eighteenth century, tea represented almost 50 percent of the company's income, while the import duties collected on tea by the British government added up to a rather astonishing 6 percent of England's national budget.

Tea was popular long before the British discovered it. About five thousand years ago in the mountains of southwest China, in what is now the province of Yunnan, humans first began drinking a liquid made from the leaves of the tea plant. The early Chinese drank the beverage—which was variously known as *ch'a*, *hsuan*, *yu*, or *té*, depending on the region in which

AUSPICIO·REGIS·ET·SENATUS·ANGLIÆ

Coat of arms for the East India Company

one lived—mainly for medicinal purposes, as a kind of bitter, leafy soup. By the seventh century BCE, the famous philosopher Laozi was calling tea "the froth of the liquid jade," showing just how valued it had become as a pleasurable drink in Chinese households and how far brewing techniques had advanced. (By this point, people had discovered that steaming the leaves immediately after picking them reduced the bitter taste.)

Tea was a popular trade item on what was known as the Ancient Tea-Horse Road, a route that stretched for thousands of miles from Sichuan and Yunnan provinces to Tibet; in its influence, this network rivaled that of the famous Silk Road. To simplify transportation, traders pressed dried tea leaves into bricks, making them a form of edible currency. The consumption of tea then spread to Japan, Southeast Asia, India, Persia, and, finally, Europe. Western audiences first read about it in 1559 in Venetian writer Giambattista Ramusio's book *Delle navigationi e viaggi* (Voyages and Travels), in which the drink is referred to as *chai catai* (tea of China) and touted as a cure for "headache, stomachache, pain in the side or in the joints." Soon, the Dutch and Portuguese began a lucrative trade in tea, introducing it to continental Europe as an expensive curative; it was sometimes brewed in huge barrels at the local apothecary, where it could be stored for months at a time.

The East India Company entered the tea trade in September 1658 with an experiment, importing a measly 140 pounds into England. Despite the paltry shipment, the drink caught on with amazing speed, due in part to the familiarity of King Charles II and his wife, Portuguese-born Catherine of Braganza, with the beverage. (Charles had grown up in exile at The Hague during the years when Oliver Cromwell ruled England.) Catherine drank it for breakfast (as a refined alternative to the gallon of beer Queen Elizabeth had traditionally downed with her morning meat and bread), and the royal couple made tea drinking popular among the wealthy elites. Soon the plant-based beverage was woven into the fabric of English middle- and upper-class life.

British colonists in Massachusetts began brewing tea around 1670. They favored a variety known as Bohea (pronounced *bo-hee*), a distortion of the name of the region in China from which it came. Bohea was essentially a "scrap tea," made up of shreds of pekoe and souchong boiled into a headily caffeinated black brew. If feeling flush, a colonist might buy Hyson, an expensive variety of green tea—but this premium product came with a measure of risk. Just as today's drug dealers will often "cut" heroin with such questionable substances as baby powder, unscrupulous eighteenth-century tea vendors would sometimes "bulk" Hyson with ingredients like sheep dung or hawthorn (the latter capable of causing cardiac arrhythmia and dangerously low blood pressure). To make the tea appear greener, poisonous dyes like copper carbonate and lead chromate might be added.

TEA AND THE COMPANY

In these early years of tea consumption, confusion reigned among colonists about the best preparation methods. According to William H. Ukers's classic history *All About Tea*, colonists in Salem, Massachusetts, would boil the leaves "for a long time, until a bitter decoction was produced, which was drunk without milk or sugar; then the leaves were salted and eaten with butter." In other provincial American towns, no pretense was made of drinking the tea liquid at all; it was simply thrown away, after which the leaves were consumed with relish.

Leave it to colonial ladies to set things aright. Taking a cue from their contemporaries in England, they began meeting over tea and elevated the drink into a social ritual. Since porcelain wares were often scarce, each guest would bring her own cup, spoon, and saucer. (In the seventeenth century, teacups lacked handles, in the Chinese fashion, and held about three ounces; by the late eighteenth century, they had evolved into the decorated porcelain vessels with handles that we know today.) A good hostess might provide several tea tables, each presenting a different type. At the very least, she would have her canisters marked *B* (to indicate that it contained Bohea or black tea), *G* (for green tea), and *S* (for sugar). From these, she would either parcel out separate teas or create her own blend.

It's not an overstatement to compare tea in the eighteenth-century colonies to coffee in twenty-first-century America—it was Everyman's morning Starbucks, Everywoman's afternoon pick-me-up, every person's after-dinner beverage of choice.

But the colonists' love affair with tea was about to come to an abrupt halt.

For the first 150 years, the colonists had it pretty easy. Unlike the Indians or the Irish or even the British back home, settlers in the new world were seldom taxed directly by the British Crown. And when England did try to impose a tax—such as the Molasses Act of 1733—local British officials were so inefficient at collecting the monies that almost everyone ignored the laws. British statesman Edmund Burke called this "salutary neglect," and the system generally worked for all considered: the British had a thriving mercantile trade with the colonies, and the colonies developed their own political and economic systems largely independent of those overseas.

Everything changed with the passage of the Sugar Act, in 1764. Parliament had recently suffered enormous financial losses to emerge victorious from the Seven Years' War (French and Indian War). Coffers were low, and Parliament decided that Americans needed to start paying their own way. The Sugar Act was designed to raise revenues for the British Crown by strictly enforcing existing customs duties as well as by placing (and collecting) an even higher duty on molasses, the prime ingredient in rum. The result was the near smothering of the molasses-rum trade, one of New England's biggest businesses.

On the heels of the Sugar Act came the next year's Stamp

BOHEA, THE COLONISTS' FAVORITE TEA, WAS GROWN IN THE WUYI MOUNTAINS OF CHINA.

By the eighteenth century, tea parties represented the height of sophistication. Note the handleless cups, in the Chinese style.

Act, a far more direct consumer tax that required all legal documents, permits, commercial contracts, newspapers, and even playing cards to carry a tax stamp. The effect of this heavy-handed legislation was not only economic but emotional, for now the stamp of the Crown would appear on almost every aspect of the life of an American colonist, from the morning paper to the deck used to play an evening's game of whist.

The Stamp Act hurt all the colonies, but Massachusetts was the first to erupt in angry protests. The reason was due, in part, to the long history in Boston (as in London) of semisanctioned gang violence. Every year on November 5, armies of young men from the North End and South End would celebrate "Pope's Day," the American equivalent of Guy Fawkes Day, by engaging in epic street brawls. Several hundreds (sometimes thousands) of young apprentices would meet in town and beat one another to a pulp, all for the sake of determining which side of town would receive bragging rights for the next year. As part of the festivities, they would burn effigies of the Devil, the pope, and other more topical scapegoats—British customs officials, British naval officers who tried to impress locals into the Royal Navy, local merchants who favored the Crown a little too slavishly—all such figures were vilified with chants and curses.

As radical leaders have discovered throughout history, a good mob is a potent tool in revolution. The leader of the South End mob was a shoemaker and firefighter by the name of

EXAMPLES OF TAX STAMPS USED ON COLONIAL MERCHANDISE

Ebenezer Mackintosh. He was so enraged by the Stamp Act that he decided to marshal his troops in political protest, and, on August 14, 1765, he led several thousand young men to Hanover Square in South Boston. There they gathered around a huge old elm tree—that had been planted in 1646—and hung an effigy of Andrew Oliver, the distributor of stamps in Massachusetts. (From that moment on, the elm was known among colonists as the Liberty Tree; later, many towns in the colonies demarked "liberty trees" or "liberty poles" of their own, symbols of support for the fight against tyranny.) That same day, Mackintosh and his mob ransacked Oliver's home and attacked and nearly destroyed the residence of Thomas Hutchinson, lieutenant governor of Massachusetts as well as Oliver's brother-in-law. Within three days, Oliver stood under the Liberty Tree and publicly resigned.

We know now that Mackintosh's famous protest wasn't directed by him alone. The plan had been either helped or fully orchestrated by a secret group of lawyers, doctors, and radical merchants who called themselves the Loyal Nine. Featured prominently among this group was Samuel Adams, the firebrand organizer whom Thomas Hutchinson sarcastically called "His Incendiary in Chief." A stout man, forty-three years old in 1765, Adams was the soft-spoken but determined son of a brewer who had tried unsuccessfully to start his own brewery, gone into debt and lost the business, and even become a tax collector for Massachusetts (although not a very good one, having accrued more than £8,000 in uncollected taxes). Even though his hands trembled with palsy, Adams was unswerving in his radical desire to keep the British Parliament from taxing the colonists.

Many historians believe that Adams and other members of the Loyal Nine convinced or secretly coerced Mackintosh into his Stamp Act–related violence; evidence exists that Adams, in his role as tax collector, sued Mackintosh for £12 in back taxes in July of 1765 and then never collected the money. After the protests, one Loyal Nine member, radical merchant Henry Bass, wrote: "We do everything in order to keep this . . . private, and are not a little pleased to hear that Mackintosh has the credit of the whole affair."

Mackintosh later experienced a falling-out with the radical patriots—he was hard to control and may have threatened to inform on them to the British—and he eventually fled Massachusetts for New Hampshire, where he died in obscurity in 1816 (his tombstone identifies him incorrectly as Philip Mackintosh). Nevertheless, his protests provided an example for lower-class Bostonians, showing them an effective way to fight against British rule.

After 1765, the Loyal Nine expanded to form a larger group called the Sons of Liberty, whose name comes from a speech made in Parliament by Isaac Barre in which the Irish politician and sympathizer of the American cause referred to patriots as "these sons of liberty." The organization later spread from Boston to New York and from there to every other colony; soon each patriotic city and hamlet had its own chapter of

Samuel Adams

"Sons," with many famous founding fathers (including John Adams, John Hancock, Paul Revere, Patrick Henry, and Benedict Arnold) counted among their ranks.

In the wake of the Boston protests, the British government repealed the Stamp Act, although the year 1768 brought a new approach to taxation known collectively as the Townshend Acts. In some ways, this legislation was less onerous than the Stamp Act, for it introduced a series of duties on a host of common imports (including paints, oils, lead, glass, and tea) rather than taxing consumer purchases (such as newspapers or playing cards). Still, the Townshend Acts sent an unmistakable message to the colonists: Great Britain could tax its colonies as much as it wanted, whenever it wanted.

Sam Adams and the Sons of Liberty responded by boycotting all goods arriving from Great Britain—especially tea. Colonists may have depended on different things for survival or financial success—some needed paints; others, glass—but they all coveted tea. Would-be consumers were constantly informed, via broadsides and patriotic newspapers, that tea was a "vile weed," a "nauseous draught," a "detestable herb." Patriots threw up the example of Dr. Samuel Johnson, the famous English lexicographer, almost sixty years old at the time, who supposedly loved tea so much "that whenever it appeared," according to one writer, "he was almost raving" mad. (An amused Dr. Johnson would answer back indirectly in a journal article, wherein he described himself sarcastically as "a hardened and shameless tea drinker. . . whose kettle has scarcely time to cool.")

The average colonist was probably too smart to believe such hyperbole, but most felt (and bowed to) the incredible social pressure exerted on them to relinquish purchasing goods taxed by the Townshend Acts. The boycott alarmed English merchants so greatly that, in 1770, Parliament repealed all the Townshend duties except a tax of threepence on—what else?—tea.

The response in America was mixed. While some colonists celebrated another successful effort to resist taxes imposed from afar, others resented the tax on their beloved beverage, trifling though it was, believing that it signified Britain's continued assertion that Americans could be taxed without their consent.

In fact, many colonists were getting their Bohea fix from smuggled teas shipped into the many hidden coves and remote beaches along the eastern coast; these contraband herbs were received by colonial middlemen, who passed them on to itinerant peddlers and shopkeepers. The smuggled goods were cheaper than teas offered for sale by the British, although the quality sometimes varied; what's more, the contraband was purchased openly. Thomas Hutchinson, governor of the colony of Massachusetts after 1770, estimated that almost three-quarters of America's "prodigious consumption" of tea was purchased on the black market. Some historians estimate that smuggled tea amounted to as much as 90 percent of the total brought into the colonies in the years before the revolution. It was also popular in Great Britain, where smugglers imported some seven million pounds annually, at great cost to the East India Company's market share.

In the early 1770s, these smugglers became the target of East India reprisals. By this time, the company was thoroughly rife with corruption, its directors retiring rich and knighted after a career of pocketing bribes; other administrators oversaw the heavy taxation of regions in India under the company's care. (A famine in Bengal in the fall of 1769 had resulted in the deaths from starvation of more than one million people, all while company directors stockpiled grain for their own use and raised taxes on the suffering local population.) In 1772, when a bank recession rocked England, the company found itself unable to borrow more money, and it was already in debt to the Bank of England to the tune of £300,000. Worse still, it owed more than £1 million in customs duties and annual payments to the English government. The only way out of the predicament, it seemed, was tea. East India had imported 17.5 million pounds into England, and this fortune in Hyson and Bohea was now sitting in warehouses with nowhere to go. After much pleading by company directors, Parliament agreed to bail them out and passed the Tea Act in 1773, allowing the EIC to export tea directly to the American colonies without paying any of the taxes it customarily delivered to the British government. (Adding insult to injury, Parliament also handed the company a £1.4 million loan.)

TEA AND THE COMPANY

This arrangement suited all relevant parties in Great Britain. The Tea Act allowed the East India Company to handpick the distributors in America with whom it wished to work, rather than selling to any American merchants who showed up for the twice-yearly tea auction in London. Although the British prime minister, Lord North, refused to rescind the threepence-per-pound tea tax (yielding to colonial will was out of the question), the new EIC tea entering America would still be cheaper than the smuggled tea. It was assumed, therefore, that colonists would simply swallow the tax along with the tea. The price of Bohea was set at two shillings a pound, which was about seven pence less than the price of smuggled tea of the same quality. "Men," Lord North wrote, "will always go to the cheapest markets."

The colonists disagreed. "They have no idea that any people can act from any principle but that of [self-] interest," Benjamin Franklin wrote to his friend Thomas Cushing, "and they believe that threepence on a pound of tea, of which one does not drink perhaps ten pounds a year, is sufficient to overcome the patriotism of an American." Colonists like Franklin were particularly upset that the threepenny tax was earmarked to pay the salaries of the very colonial administrators they considered oppressors (Governor Hutchinson among them). Colonial merchants were enraged, too, that the East India Company had effectively cut them out of the supply chain, awarding huge shares of the market to Loyalist merchants who toadied up to the ogres overseas.

TEN TEA PARTIES

While Americans seethed in the summer of 1773, East India picked the consignees in American ports who would receive the company's tea. In Boston these included two sons of Governor Hutchinson, Thomas Jr. and Elisha; Benjamin Faneuil, a member of a wealthy Loyalist family; and Richard Clarke, a merchant who just happened to be Governor Hutchinson's nephew. These selections made it clear to American onlookers that only those with strong Loyalist connections need apply.

In September and October, the EIC stocked a total of 544,000 pounds of tea—roughly two thousand full chests—and loaded them aboard seven sturdy trading ships. Setting sail for Boston were the *Eleanor, Dartmouth, William,* and *Beaver*; the *Nancy* was destined for New York, the *Polly* for Philadelphia, and the *London* for Charleston, South Carolina.

The East India Company was blanketing America's four major ports (and the cities harboring the most tea smugglers) with its new, low-priced product. The directors had to practice patience first—a voyage across the Atlantic could take from four to eight weeks, depending on the weather—but they believed that as soon as their tea arrived, it would radically transform the current market in America, make the colonists happy, and restore the fortunes of the East India Company.

Of course, it didn't quite work out that way.

CHAPTER TWO

The Boston
Tea Party

December 1773

"The hour of destruction,
or manly opposition to the
machinations of tyranny,
stares you in the face."

From a handbill posted in Boston, 1773

O n October 18, 1773, the *Boston Gazette*—the newspaper of record for patriots, although locals loyal to the king called it "the weekly dung barge"—announced that thousands of pounds of the cheap Bohea was wending its way toward Boston. The tidbit was not what one would call flattering:

> It is the current Talk of the Town that Richard Clarke, Benjamin Faneuil, and the two young Messers Hutchinson are appointed to receive the Tea allowed to be exported to this place. This new scheme of Administration lately said to be so friendly to the Colonies, is at once so threatening to the trade, and so well calculated to establish and encrease the detested TRIBUTE, that an attempt to meddle with this pernicious Drug would render men much more respected than they are . . . obnoxious.

The remainder of the notice made it clear that the Sons of Liberty would prohibit the tea from being unloaded in Boston. And this notice was the first of many such warnings. On Tuesday, November 2, tea consignee Richard Clarke—nephew and close friend of Governor Hutchinson—was awakened at one o'clock in the morning by a loud pounding on his front door. He sent a servant to answer it. The man returned with a note that read: "The Freemen of this Province understand, from good authority, that there is a quantity of tea assigned to your house by the East India Company. . . . It is therefore expected that you personally appear at the Liberty Tree on Wednesday next, at twelve o'clock noon, to make public resignation of your commission. . . . Fail not upon your peril."

The note was signed "O. C.," initials that almost certainly stood for Oliver Cromwell, the seventeenth-century Puritan rebel who had overthrown the British Crown and executed King Charles I. Cromwell was so hated by Royalists that, after their return to power, they dug up his corpse and had it beheaded. Naturally, this hated radical served as an inspiration to the American patriots.

When Clarke conferred with his fellow assignees, he learned they all had received the same note. And none had any intention of standing under the Liberty Tree and submitting to a public humiliation. As far as the men were concerned, they were guilty of only one thing: accepting a profitable commission that their fellow patriot-merchants would have given their eyeteeth to get. Besides, they had already signed an agreement with the East India Company and thus were contractually bound to receive the shipment. Business was business.

When the bells of Boston struck twelve on the morning of November 3, calling the crowd to the Liberty Tree, Clarke and his fellow merchants were conspicuously absent. "You may well judge that none of us ever entertained the least thoughts of obeying the summons," Clarke would later write to a friend, especially since the mob of about five hundred men that eventually gathered around the tree consisted chiefly of "people of the lowest rank." And though it's true that the group had its share of well-muscled apprentice agitators—the heart of any Boston mob—it also included Samuel Adams, John Hancock, Paul Revere, and militant patriot Joseph Warren. A group of Boston radicals called the North End Caucus was also present and hung a flag of protest from the ancient branches of the esteemed Liberty Tree. (Interestingly enough, the flag was a Union Jack, which protesting patriots had hung on the old elm's great branches since 1765. This choice of standard would continue until the shooting war began in 1775, serving as a way for even radical patriots to claim that such protests were directed against the policies of a few corrupt London politicians and businessmen, not against Great Britain as a whole.)

As the hours passed with no sign of Clarke or the other

consignees, the crowd beneath the elm grew increasingly agitated. There was talk of seeking the men out and forcefully bringing them to the Liberty Tree. The crowd's chants and shouts could be heard from blocks away.

With their anxiety increasing by the minute, the consignees spent most of the day behind locked doors. After communicating via messenger, they decided to meet at Clarke's warehouse, accompanied by a dozen strong young men they had enlisted as bodyguards. There they huddled in an upper-story room to try to figure out how, as Clarke would later describe it, "to oppose the designs of the mob."

Their plan had just one problem. Someone (perhaps a trusted bodyguard) had leaked their location to the crowd gathered beneath the Liberty Tree. The crowd then elected nine delegates to go to the warehouse and demand the consignees' presence at the predetermined location. These nine were followed by a few dozen members of the mob; the crowd waited outside a nearby tavern (and likely enjoyed a drink or two) while the delegates barged into the building and made their way up to the second floor to confront Clarke and his fellow merchants.

The meeting was short. William Molineux, leader of the delegates, read aloud a paper that he ordered the consignees to sign—it contained a promise not to unload the tea or to pay duty on it. When Clarke refused, Molineux informed him that the merchants "must expect to feel the utmost weight of the people's resentment" as "enemies to their country."

This was no idle phrase. As soon as Molineux and the others conveyed Clarke's refusal to the crowd waiting outdoors, the "utmost weight of the people"—in the form of a dozen shouting (and, by now, possibly drunk) patriots—rushed the warehouse. The men ripped the front door off its hinges and piled up the narrow staircase to the second floor. The consignees' burly backers repelled the mob with fists, bloodying a few noses in the process. After a scrambling melee, which saw several people shoved off the stairs, the crowd eventually gave up and emptied onto the streets.

That night, Clarke and the other consignees received yet another threatening note, which concluded with still more dire words: "Remember, gentlemen, this is the last warning you are ever to expect from the insulted, abused, and most indignant vindicators of violated liberty in the Town of Boston."

Now, if you were a Loyalist, the events of November third were bad news, indeed. None of the tea ships had even arrived in Boston Harbor, and yet the city had already erupted into violence. The day after the confrontation at the warehouse, a patriot newspaper warned of the "danger of lives being lost." The implication was clear: those who chose to support the importation of East India Company tea were risking their lives.

But, from Samuel Adams's point of view, things were proceeding along swimmingly. Then fifty-one years old, Adams had been advocating for and writing in defense of American independence ever since those first early Stamp Act protests. He hadn't always had an easy time of it; after the repeal of the Townshend Acts, many Bostonians had been willing to relax their vigilance against Great Britain. Yet Adams continued to work furiously to stir up more discontent, taking advantage of violent incidents against Boston street agitators—such as the Boston Massacre of 1770, in which harassed British soldiers opened fire on an angry mob, killing five—to agitate against the Crown. Moreover, Adams was unswerving in his manipulation of all those who might help him achieve his goals, including John Hancock, a merchant whose great wealth helped bankroll the Sons of Liberty. (One Loyalist writer lampooned Hancock as "Johnny Dupe, Esq.")

On November 5, Pope's Day, Adams called a meeting of more than one thousand at Faneuil Hall—the meeting hall donated to the town, ironically enough, by Peter Faneuil, father of Benjamin—where it was again resolved that the consignees must refuse their tea shipments. Once again, a delegation was sent to Clarke and his fellow merchants, who remained obstinate. Governor Hutchinson, an observer of the situation, wrote to his superior, the Earl of Dartmouth, that "at present the spirits of the people of Boston are in great ferment." But there was nothing he could do about it, he complained, because the people of Boston responded not to him but to a shadow government run by Samuel Adams. Things grew so tense that, one by one, the consignees, with the exception of Clarke, fled the city—fearful, as they said, of losing their lives to the men they called the "Sons of Violence."

Violence did in fact erupt again, on November 17, when a mob of several hundred, blowing whistles and shouting insults, approached the home of Richard Clarke. When no one went out to meet them, they rushed the house and pounded on the locked front door, so enraging one of Clarke's sons that the young man raced to an upstairs window and fired a pistol at the crowd, supposedly shouting: "You rascals! Be gone or I'll blow your brains out!" Fortunately, the shot hit no one—the gun may have been loaded with powder instead of lead—but the mob naturally took this affront amiss. They proceeded to attack the house, according to the elder Clarke, "with stones, brickbats, clubs, and cord wood . . . for the space of two hours," breaking windows and terrifying the family. For Richard Clarke, it was the last straw. On November 23, he fled to the countryside while his sons remained in the city to try to negotiate a settlement.

At last, on November 28, the first shipment arrived in Boston. The *Dartmouth*, carrying 114 chests of tea, anchored off Fort William, on Castle Island (later the Boston headquarters of the British army during the Revolutionary War). The next morning, patriotic handbills appeared all over the city:

> Friends! Brethren! Countrymen!—That worst of plagues, the detested tea, shipped for this port by the East India Company, is now arrived in the harbor; the hour of destruction, or manly opposition to the machinations of tyranny, stares you in the face.

Also that morning, Samuel Adams convened an assembly at Faneuil Hall. Because so many people showed up (including representatives from four nearby towns), the gathering had to be moved to Old South Church, the largest meeting place in Boston. The church, normally unheated and freezing inside at the end of November, was packed to the choir loft. It's doubtful any of the attendees were shivering.

All present reaffirmed that the tea would not be allowed to be unloaded onto land—and no duties would be paid on it. Instead, it would be returned to England in the very same ships that had brought it to Boston. These demands were delivered by messenger to the ship's consignees, who were given until three o'clock to agree to the terms. While waiting for the reply, the crowds that had gathered in Old South Church cheered speeches delivered by Adams and other Sons of Liberty. There was much talk of "blood shed" if the consignees tried to land the tea.

Rather than replying to the demands, the consignees fled, either to Castle Island or to the homes of friends. A full two days passed before their counteroffer was delivered: The men stated that, because of their signed agreements with the East India Company, they could not be "Active instruments" in returning the tea; to do so would ruin them financially. They would, however, be willing to place the tea in temporary storage while negotiations continued over its fate.

Adams, Hancock, and the rest of the Sons of Liberty were not impressed, and they declared the offer unacceptable. Placing the tea in temporary storage meant removing it from the ship, and anyone caught trying to do so would face dire consequences.

In the meantime, two royal customs officers had boarded the *Dartmouth*, an event that increased pressure on the consignees and the Sons of Liberty alike. One of the arcane laws of the era stated that, once a king's customs official had inspected a cargo, the owner of said cargo had twenty days to unload it, pay applicable duties (in this case, the reviled threepence tax), and cart it away. If no one claimed the cargo within twenty days—for the *Dartmouth's* tea, by December 17—the goods would be seized by the local governor and sold at auction, under armed guard if necessary, with the proceeds split between the governor and the customs office.

The consignees understood that unloading the tea was a lost cause—blood would certainly be shed if they tried—and instead they opted to risk financial ruin. And so it was left to Adams and the Sons of Liberty to take the next step. They knew they could not allow the "accursed" tea to go to auction on December 17.

THE TEA SHIP "DARTMOUTH" ANCHORED IN BOSTON HARBOR

The valuable load would attract plenty of takers, and they worried that a sale would undermine all their efforts. But what, exactly, could they do with it?

In a remarkable demonstration of power, Adams ordered the *Dartmouth* moved from Castle Island to Griffin's Wharf, a long outdoor dock equipped with a partial roof. As the other ships arrived, they, too, were to be tied there. The *Eleanor* made land on December 3, and the *Beaver* followed on December 7; the *William*, which had run aground on Cape Cod, never reached Boston. The ships, unloaded of all cargo except the tea, sat and swayed at their moorings, guarded by a gang of grim-looking patriots. Rumors ran wild: that his majesty's soldiers were lining up a huge 42-pound cannon to fire on Griffin's Wharf, that redcoats were mustering to attack the town.

As the fateful date approached, the Boston Sons of Liberty were on the receiving end of still more pressure, this time from patriots in Philadelphia, New York, and Charleston, all of whom were expecting their own East India Company tea shipments to arrive in the coming weeks. Everyone was looking to Boston to set the example: Would the colonists yield and allow the tea to be set on land? A plaintive complaint, from a letter written by one Philadelphia radical, was published in the *Boston Gazette*: "All that we fear, is that you will shrink at Boston . . . we fear you will suffer this to be landed." A newspaper from New York echoed the sentiment: "If you touch one grain of this accursed tea, you are undone. America is threatened with worse than Egyptian slavery."

On December 14, Adams and the Sons of Liberty made one last effort to return the tea to London. Despite being certain that he was acting honorably, Adams wanted to appear to be taking every possible means to resolve the situation lawfully. He convinced Francis Rotch, the owner of the *Dartmouth*, to try to obtain a clearance waiver from Governor Hutchinson; such a document would allow him to ship the tea back to England without paying the requisite duty.

On the cold and rainy afternoon of December 16, a crowd of more than five thousand gathered once again in Boston's Old South Church, in what was to date the largest town meeting in the city's history. And, once again, attendees packed the church to the rafters, crowding together to stay warm; as the dreary afternoon wore on, candles were lit to illuminate the various speakers. Those unable to fit inside the building huddled outside beneath the windows, listening to speeches and gathering updates. While they waited for Rotch to return from his visit with Hutchinson, the assembled group learned that the nearby town of Lexington had, in a show of solidarity, gathered all its tea and publicly burned it. (This act thus gives Lexington the distinction of staging America's first tea party; see page 205.) When the news was announced, the crowd erupted in a raucous cheer.

Rotch returned with the news that Hutchinson refused to

budge: he would not allow the ships to leave without unloading their cargoes of tea. Those in attendance began shouting their own ideas for how to respond. Some wanted to haul the ships out of the water, drag them to Boston Common, and burn them. Others suggested torching the vessels right at the wharf. But Adams, Hancock, and the Sons of Liberty had been expecting just this news, and they had already set a backup plan in motion. Even as Rotch relayed his report to the assembly, a few dozen young men were slipping out the door and darting through the city's wintry alleyways.

More speakers rose to address the audience, and various proposals were weighed and considered. Debate reigned. But if there was agreement about anything, it was this: the situation was about to get very, very ugly. In a moment of prescience, patriot Josiah Quincy warned that the coming events were likely to "bring on the most trying & terrible struggle this country ever saw."

When Quincy had finished speaking, John Adams rose suddenly and announced: "This meeting can do nothing more to save this country." At that very moment, the assembly heard war whoops coming from the street. A band of about thirty young men, appearing, as one writer reported, "to be Aboriginal Natives from their complection," materialized in the church's front doorway. The timing was so precise that some historians believe Adams's statement was in fact a signal for the "Indians" to arrive.

Someone inside the church shouted, "The Mohawks are come!" and the crowd poured out to watch what would happen next.

A few of the so-called Mohawks were the same young men who had slipped away during Francis Rotch's delivery of his bad news. Most were apprentices selected for the job by the Sons of Liberty and organized with military precision into squads; in carpentry shops and back rooms of printing establishments and in the homes of their employers, these men had waited for a signal. By the time the call came, their disguises had been donned. Of course, no one truly mistook them for Mohawks. They wore ragged clothes, hoods, and blankets thrown over their heads; they painted their faces with ochre and lampblack. It's not entirely clear why they chose to masquerade as Indians. Perhaps the disguise was easiest to generate on last-minute notice, or perhaps it was a way to illustrate their Yankee identity and further distinguish themselves from the British. Whatever the reason, one thing is certain: none was wearing the types of elaborate costumes and feathered headdresses depicted in many illustrations of the Boston Tea Party. Still, they certainly did whoop and holler and generally whipped the bystanders into a frenzy.

There were shouts from several people in the crowd who were obviously aware of what the Sons of Liberty had been planning: "Boston Harbor a tea pot tonight!" "Who knows how tea will mingle with salt water!" "Hurrah for Griffin's Wharf!" The Indians proceeded to the harbor, the crowd following along. One bystander would later write, "You'd thought that inhabitants of the infernal regions had broken loose."

Despite later rumors to the contrary, Sam Adams, John Hancock, and other prominent (and highly recognizable) patriots did not participate in the events that night. They had set the Tea Party in motion, and now it was time for the "people of the lowest rank" to carry it off. Led by the Mohawks, the crowd marched to Griffin's Wharf. The core group of thirty disguised patriots was joined by another fifty to one hundred or so young men who smeared soot or coal dust on their faces as an impromptu disguise. Today's readers might be surprised to learn just how young some of these men were; the crowd included a fifteen-year-old blacksmith's apprentice named Joshua Wyeth and thirteen-year-old Peter Slater, an apprentice rope maker. Some were acting under the direct orders of their masters; others were apprenticed to Loyalists but had sneaked out to participate in the hoopla.

The rain had stopped, the night had turned colder, and the thin sliver of a new moon could be seen overhead. After the tumult of the meeting, the crowd had grown quiet, as though those present understood they were watching something momentous take place. Participants carried torches and lanterns that, according to one bystander, "made everything as light as day." As they reached the wharf, they could see the three tea-laden ships moored silently in the water. Beyond them, anchored in the harbor, stood the darkened silhouettes of British warships, the sight of which gave more than one of the patriots pause. The Sons of Liberty did not expect the British to take action against the protestors—a large-scale bloodbath was the last thing the government wanted. Nevertheless, the Mohawks took the precaution of surrounding themselves with what one British officer described as "the Body of the People who had been at the meeting"—in other words, a human shield.

When the protestors reached the harbor, the shield fell away and the Mohawks walked alone onto Griffin's Wharf. There they divided into three previously determined groups and each boarded one of the ships: the *Dartmouth*, the *Eleanor*, and the *Beaver*. On board the *Beaver*, a young cobbler named George R.T. Hewes was dispatched by Lendall Pitts, the "commander" of his "division," to approach the captain, a man named Coffin, and ask for the keys to the hatches that led down to the hold as well as a dozen candles. The captain complied but begged that no damage be done to his ship or its non-tea cargo. (Quarantined for a few days because of a smallpox outbreak, the vessel had yet to unload its other consignments.) Hewes summoned Pitts, who promised that if Coffin "would go into his cabin quietly, not one article of his goods would be hurt." The same scene played out on the other two vessels; the tea destroyers were incredibly disciplined and true to their word. When a padlock was accidentally broken on the *Dartmouth*, a new one was brought to the ship the next day.

THE BOSTON TEA PARTY

Schoolbook accounts of the Boston Tea Party often depict whooping Indians laughing and tossing tea into the sea, but, in truth, the task was physically exhausting. The three ships contained a total of 342 chests stocked with tea. Most chests weighed four hundred pounds apiece, and each had to be lifted from the holds using block and tackle equipment borrowed from the ships. Once the chests were raised, the men attacked them with axes, hatchets, and clubs, but the strokes of their blades were blunted by the heavy canvas covering the chests. Opened chests were dragged to the railings and the tea was dumped overboard, after which the chests were smashed to bits and the pieces tossed in the harbor as well. One of the protestors, a blacksmith used to physical exertion, recalled: "I never labored harder in my life."

Because the harbor was at low tide, the ships rested in only a few feet of water and the large quantities of tea dumped overboard refused to sink. Massive hills of pungent leaves floated in the mucky water like giant haystacks; one pile grew so big that it toppled back onto the ship from which it had been thrown. Soon protestors were assigned to jump into the shallows and rake the tea as they would freshly mown hay.

Of course, a few folks couldn't resist stuffing a little contraband into their pockets. Indeed, the craven colonist seeking a few ounces of free Bohea is a recurring character in nearly all the tea parties described in this book. Young Hewes caught one man filling his pockets and the lining of his coat. "Just as he was stepping

Tea
that was gathered up on the
Shore of Dorchester neck on
the morning after the destruction
of the three Cargoes at Boston
December 17. 1773

Tea leaves recovered from the Boston Tea Party

down from the vessel, I seized him by the skirt of his coat and in attempting to pull him back I tore it off." The man, a Captain O'Connor, got away, but the next day Hewes nailed his coat to the whipping post in town as a reminder of what awaited him should he show his face. Other would-be tea thieves embarked in canoes and paddled up to the piles, but they were driven off with oaths and punches by protestors waiting in the water for just such attempts.

By nine o'clock, the Boston Tea Party had run its course. Within the span of a few hours the men had destroyed 92,600 pounds of tea, an astonishing amount worth more than £9,659 at the time (perhaps as much as $1 million in today's currency). The decks of the ships were swept clean, and the leavings dumped overboard. When the men lined up on the wharf, their commanders ordered them to shake out their shoes and empty their pockets, after which any tea scraps were swept into the harbor. (Despite such thoroughness, not quite all the tea was destroyed that night. A young protestor named Thomas Mevill, grandfather to the great American novelist Herman Melville, found some in his shoe and placed it in a bottle, which is preserved to this day at the Old State House Museum in Boston.)

After dusting themselves off, the protestors marched away with military discipline and the crowds of spectators dispersed. Back on the streets of Boston, Lendall Pitts's troop passed by the window of a prominent Loyalist who happened to be entertaining

T E A,

DESTROYED BY INDIANS.

YE GLORIOUS SONS OF FREEDOM, brave and bold,
    That has stood forth----fair LIBERTY to hold ;
Though you were INDIANS, come from distant shores,
Like MEN you acted-----not like savage Moors.

CHORUS.

Bostonian's SONS keep up your Courage good,
Or Dye, like Martyrs, in fair Free-born Blood.

Our LIBERTY, and LIFE is now invaded,
And FREEDOM's brightest Charms are darkly shaded ;
But, we will STAND---and think it noble mirth,
To DART the man that dare oppress the Earth.

Bostonian's SONS keep up your Courage good,
Or Dye, like Martyrs, in fair Free-born Blood.

How grand the Scene !----(No Tyrant shall oppose)
The T E A is sunk in spite of all our foes.
A NOBLE SIGHT---to see th' accursed T E A
Mingled with MUD----and ever for to be ;
For KING and PRINCE shall know that we are FREE.

Bostonian's SONS keep up your Courage good,
Or Dye, like Martyrs, in fair Free-born Blood,

Must we be still--- and live on Blood-bought Ground,
And not oppose the Tyrants cursed found ?
We Scorn the thought----our views are well refin'd
We Scorn those slavish shackles of the Mind,
" We've Souls that were not made to be confin'd."

Bostonian's SONS keep up your Courage good,
Or Dye, like Martyrs, in fair Free-born Blood.

Could our Fore-fathers rise from their cold Graves,
And view their Land, with all their Children SLAVES
What would they say ! how would their Spirits rend,
And, Thunder-strucken, to their Graves descend.

Bostonian's SONS keep up your Courage good,
Or Dye, like Martyrs, in fair Free-born Blood.

Let us with hearts of steel now stand the tast,
Throw off all darksome ways, nor wear a Mask.
Oh ! may our noble Zeal support our frame,
And brand all Tyrants with eternal SHAME.

Bostonian's SONS keep up your Courage good,
And sink all Tyrants in their GUILTY BLOOD.

AMERICAN BROADSIDE PRAISING "YE GLORIOUS SONS OF FREEDOM"

FOR RAIDING THE BRITISH TEA SHIPS

THE BOSTON TEA PARTY

Admiral John Montagu, commander of Great Britain's North American squadron. Perhaps frustrated for not being allowed to unleash his warships on the tea destroyers, Montagu opened the window and shouted: "Well, boys, you've had a fine, pleasant evening with your Indian caper, haven't you? But mind, you've got to pay the fiddler yet!"

To which Pitts shouted back: "Oh never mind, Squire. Just come out here, if you please, and we'll settle the bill in two minutes."

The admiral declined the invitation.

The next morning, Samuel Adams arose early and dashed off messages to Sons of Liberty chapters in New York and Philadelphia: "Every ounce of the tea on board [the tea ships] was immersed in the Bay, without the least injury to private property. The Spirit of the People on this occasion surprised all parties who viewed the Scene. We conceived it our duty to afford you the most early advice of this interesting event by express, which departing immediately obliges us to conclude."

The aforementioned "express" was none other than Paul Revere who—in a foreshadowing of his famous ride almost eighteen months later—galloped south with the dispatches. He arrived in New York on December 21. Three days later, the citizens of Philadelphia heard the news, and by mid-January the story of the Boston Tea Party had reached South Carolina and points farther south. Revere returned to Boston two days after

Christmas with the news that church bells had rung in New York and Philadelphia as patriotic citizens wildly cheered the destruction of the tea in Boston Harbor.

Meanwhile, a speedy ship was already sailing from Boston to London with the story of the shocking events at Griffin's Wharf. The news reached Parliament on January 20, 1774, and members immediately went into session to decide what punishment would be meted out to the rebellious Americans.

What none of them yet knew was that, nearly a month earlier, on Christmas Day in Philadelphia, a *second* tea party had already occurred.

CHAPTER THREE

The Philadelphia
Tea Party

December 1773

"Captain Ayres ... ought to have known our people better than to have expected we would be so mean as to suffer his rotten tea to be funneled down our throats with the Parliament's duty mixed with it."

The Committee for Tarring and Feathering

What think you, Captain, of a Halter around your Neck—ten Gallons of liquid Tar decanted on your Pate—with the Feathers of a dozen wild Geese laid over that to enliven your Appearance? Only think seriously of this—and fly to the Place from whence you came—fly without Hesitation—without the Formality of a Protest—and above all, Captain Ayres, let us advise you to fly without the wild Geese Feathers.

The above broadside was addressed to Captain Ayres of the British ship *Polly*, which was laden with 697 chests of East India Company tea and moored in Chester, Pennsylvania, a few miles south of Philadelphia, on the Delaware River. It was signed: "Your friends to serve. THE COMMIT-TEE OF TARRING AND FEATHERING." The day was December 25, 1773, and the handbill represented an unwelcome Christmas card for the weary sailor. His ship had departed London on September 27, along with the other East India Company vessels carrying tea to Boston, but adverse weather had disrupted his passage; the good captain and his crew spent almost three months aboard the tiny, bucking craft. Ayres was no doubt shaking his head grimly at the notice delivered that morning just as members of that very same Committee of Tarring and Feathering showed up on the dock, demanding to be taken aboard.

The handbill—which has that mixture of broad humor and seething menace peculiar to patriotic documents during the lead-up to the revolution—was enough to give Ayres, or anyone, serious pause. Tarring and feathering—or, as the colonists called it, "the American Exhibition"—had been practiced in Europe since medieval times, but it was a relatively new form of political protest in the colonies. The first known occurrence took place in Salem, Massachusetts, in 1768, after a crowd of patriots caught a man suspected of being a British informant. According to one contemporary account, the group "stripped him, then wrapped him in a Tarred Sheet, then rolled him in Feathers; having done this, they carried him about the Streets in a Cart and then banished him from town for six weeks."

This particular miscreant was lucky enough to be wrapped in a tarred sheet; many mobs didn't hesitate to strip a man naked and smear tar directly onto the skin. In fact, they would often heat the pine tar (plentiful in the colonies, where it was used to waterproof ships) to make the experience even more painful; if the victim suffered a few bone fractures in the process, removing the pine tar from the skin would be all the more agonizing. The cruelest variant was probably "pitchcapping," which involved covering the victim's head with tar. The substance could be removed only by yanking off all the hair, and often a good deal of the scalp as well, a disfiguring process that left behind permanent scars.

Having been at sea for months, Ayres was likely surprised by the hostile reception, especially since he was as yet unaware of the destruction of tea that had occurred in Boston. (Indeed, Philadelphians themselves had learned about the events only the day before, on December 24.) He may even have been expecting a friendly welcome—after all, Philadelphia was a city whose very name spoke of tolerance and civility. It was the City of Brotherly Love, as William Penn had so named it by combining the Greek words *philos* (love) and *adelphos* (brother).

Perhaps more to the point, Philadelphia was the American city closest to British hearts, a city they considered much more genteel than brawling Boston. A mercantile center with a population hovering around 30,000, it was also the third most important trade center in the British empire, after London and Liverpool. There was much for British visitors to admire. For one thing, the climate was not as hot and pestilent as, say, Charlestown. And residents were on relatively good terms with local native populations since, years earlier, William Penn had made a point of making peace with the Indians. Then there was the mighty Delaware, a vital waterway that transported the many exports of inland farms and forests to the city, to the ocean, and beyond.

Perhaps most beneficial to the Crown, Philadelphians were avid consumers of British imports. They dressed "according to the English fashion," as one European visitor wrote in the 1760s, and bought everything from clothing and carpets to farm equipment and furniture. Even Benjamin Franklin couldn't resist the allure of the sophisticated English merchandise; he once sent his wife, Deborah, a list of "Baubles from Britain": "a fine Piece of Pompador Sattin, 14 Yards cost 11s. per Yard. A Silk Negligee and Petticoat of brocaded Lutestring for my dear Sally, with 2 Doz. Gloves ... 3 Damask Table Cloths, a Piece of Crimson Morin for Curtains, with Tassels, Line and Binding. A large true Turkey Carpet cost 10 Guineas, for the Dining Parlour ... and a Gimcrack Corkscrew."

The shopping sprees of Franklin and hundreds of like-minded Philadelphians convinced the East India Company—along with the merchant consignees of the Philadelphia import-export firms James & Drinker, Thomas Wharton, and Jonathan Browne, which had contracted for the tea—that the 700 chests heading their way (twice as many as had arrived at Boston) would translate into enormous profits. Besides, not a single member of the Pennsylvania assembly had protested the Tea Act. Even though many merchants understood the principle

IN THIS CARTOON, COLONISTS POUR SCALDING TEA DOWN THE THROAT OF A TARRED AND FEATHERED TAX COLLECTOR.

behind the protests, they never thought Philadelphians would tolerate a boycott of the new, cheaper tea.

Residents learned of the coming shipment in early October. A handbill, posted on walls and in city taverns, announced the crisis with the headline: "By uniting we stand; by dividing we fall." The document was addressed to the merchant consignees appointed by the East India Company, and one can only suspect that such an announcement left them feeling unsettled. The rest of the document erased any doubt about the seriousness of the situation:

> You need not be surprised that the eyes of ALL are now fixed on you; as on men, who have it in their power to ward off the most dangerous stroke, that has ever been meditated against the liberties of America. . . . It is in our power and you are now warn'd of it to save YOURSELVES much trouble, and secure your native Country from the deadly Stroke now aimed in your persons against her.

It was signed *Scaevola*, the name of celebrated Roman soldier who had been taken captive and, in an act of bravery, burned his hand over a flame to show the Etruscan king that he was unafraid of torture.

But pseudonymous broadsides alone do not a revolution

make. To aid the cause, William Bradford, owner of the London Coffee House and publisher of the *Pennsylvania Journal*, stepped up to assure a group of patriots worried about failing to organize a boycott: "Leave that business to me—I'll collect a town meeting for you—prepare some resolves [and] . . . they shall be executed." Bradford used his connections and conviction to arrange a meeting with several influential Philadelphians, including Charles Thomson, Thomas Mifflin, Dr. Benjamin Rush, and Dr. Thomas Cadwalader. As in Boston, the patriots were more concerned about the East India Company's hunger for monopoly than the thruppence tax on tea (although the latter point was easier to communicate to the public). Together the men generated a list of eight resolutions:

1. That the disposal of their own property is the inherent right of freemen; that there can be no property in that which another can, of right, take from us without our consent; that the claim of parliament to tax America, is, in other words, a claim of right to levy contributions on us at pleasure.

2. That the duty, imposed by parliament upon tea landed in America, is a tax on the Americans, or levying contributions on them, without their consent.

3. That the express purpose, for which the tax is levied on the Americans, namely, for the support of government, administration of justice, and defense of his majesty's dominions in America, has a direct tendency to render assemblies useless, and to introduce arbitrary government and slavery.

4. That a virtuous and steady opposition, to this ministerial plan of governing America, is absolutely necessary, to preserve even the shadow of liberty; and is a duty which every freeman in America owes to his country, to himself, and to his posterity.

5. That the resolution, lately entered into by the East India Company, to send out their tea to America, subject to the payment of duties on its being landed here, is an open attempt to enforce this ministerial plan, and a violent attack upon the liberties of America.

6. That it is the duty of every American to oppose this attempt.

7. That whoever shall, directly or indirectly, countenance this attempt, or, in any wise, aid or abet in unloading, receiving, or vending the tea sent out by the

ADVERTISEMENT DETAILING THE "MEDLEY" OF FINE

IMPORTS AVAILABLE TO COLONISTS

East India Company, while it remains subject to the payment of a duty here, is an enemy to his country.

8. That a committee be immediately chosen, to wait on those gentlemen, who, it is reported, are appointed by the East India Company, to receive and sell said tea, and request them, from a regard to their own character and the peace and good order of the city and province, immediately to resign their appointment.

Two men who found fault with the resolutions were Abel James and Henry Drinker, of James & Drinker, the firm that was expecting a windfall in profits not only from the tea aboard *Polly* but also from all the tea the East India Company would consign to them in the future. James had already written to merchants in New York regarding the Tea Act, in which he expressed doubt that the population would raise much of a fuss: "Our private intelligencers inform us that the common people are very slow at apprehending this to be a matter of [as much importance] as the Smugglers would represent it."

Alas, James had underestimated "the common people" of Philadelphia—or at least the media's ability to rally them to a cause. In his paper, Bradford called for a town meeting to take place on October 16 "to consider what Measures will be necessary to prevent the landing of a large Quantity of TEA." He went on to assert that the approaching tea delivery represented "a VERY dangerous Attempt to render ineffectual your virtuous Exertions, against the Inroads of Oppression and Slavery."

Thousands gathered on the meeting day and voted to approve the resolves put forward by Bradford and his compatriots, thus making Philadelphia the first colonial city to publicly protest the Tea Act. The resolutions were printed in the *Philadelphia Gazette*; three weeks later, when Bostonians assembled in Faneuil Hall, they too adopted the same resolutions, saying: "That the sense of this town cannot be better expressed than in the words of certain judicious resolves, lately entered into by our worthy brethren, the citizens of Philadelphia."

Also at the meeting, attendees nominated a committee of twelve to approach James, Drinker, and the other two assignees, Wharton and Browne. The committee visited each man at home—always an effective approach—and strongly advised them to refuse the deliveries. Wharton and Browne saw the writing on the wall and immediately backed down; the former wrote to a friend, "Threats are thow'd out of destroying the Property [the tea], to such a pitch of Zeal are some People rais'd that I fear the worst."

It took a little more work to convince James and Drinker, even after a none-too-subtle newspaper article that suggested their warehouse should be built of stone (a thinly veiled threat of arson). Only when a mob showed up at the firm's place of business and confronted Abel James did he agree to refuse the tea, even swearing on the head of his young daughter Rebecca standing next to him.

All that remained was for *Polly* to reach port. In the days preceding the ship's arrival, the resolute patriots endeavored to rouse the populace against accepting the tea and paying the tax. They distributed handbills and wrote newspaper articles in a campaign that was even wider ranging (and, in some ways, more sophisticated) than the efforts undertaken by the Sons of Liberty in Boston. One such handbill declared that "if Merchants are ruined, ship building ceases," an attempt to link the monopolies of the East India Company with a collapse of the entire chain of commerce. Ministers sympathetic to the cause preached anti-tea sermons and railed against the beverage's unhealthy properties; some suggested that it encouraged the female population to be idle and gossipy. One doctor warned that women would use "Deceit and vile Stratagems"—including sexual favors—to obtain money to spend on tea, which was rumored to be a sexual aphrodisiac.

In the months leading up to the ship's arrival, some patriots expressed concern that it might sneak through the Delaware Bay and enter the port undetected. To protect against such an occurrence, they created a series of handbills and distributed them to Delaware River pilots; in them, the *Polly* and its commander are described in amusing (though still threatening) terms. One, dated December 7, reads:

> The regard we have for your characters and our desire to promote your future peace and safety are the occasion of this third address to you. In our second letter we acquainted you that the tea ship was a three decker. We are now informed by good authority she is not a three decker, but an old black ship without a Head [bowsprit] or any Ornaments.

> The Captain is a short fat Fellow, and a little obstinate withal—so much the worse for him—For, so sure as he rides rusty, We shall heave him, Keel out, and see that his Bottom be well fired, scrubbed and paid—His Upper-Works too, will have an Overhawling—and it is said he has good deal of Quick Work about him, We will take particular care that such part of him undergoes a thorough Rummaging. We have a still worse account of his owner; for it is said the ship Polly was bought by him on purpose to make a penny of us and that he and Captain Ayres were well advised of the risk they would run in thus daring to insult and abuse us.

Captain Ayres was here in the time of the Stamp Act and ought to have known our people better than to have expected we would be so mean as to suffer his rotten tea to be funneled down our throats with the Parliament's duty mixed with it.

We know him well and we have calculated to a Gill and a Feather how much it will require to fit him for an American Exhibition. And we hope not one of your Body will behave so ill, as to bilge us to clap him in the Cart along Side of the Captain.

We must repeat the SHIP POLLY is an old black Ship of some 250 tons burthen, without a head, and without ornaments, and that Captain Ayres is a thick chunky Fellow. As such, TAKE CARE to AVOID THEM.

Your Old Friends,
The Committee for Tarring and Feathering

Using words and imagery that were far different from those in the eight resolutions, but that pilots plying the Delaware would easily understand, the patriots ensured that no one would unknowingly guide the British tea ship to Philadelphia. At last, on December 25—after a night spent celebrating the news of the Boston Tea Party—word came that the *Polly* was moored at Chester, having made its way up the river from Delaware Bay. The Committee of Tarring and Feathering wasted no time in securing a boat, traveling downriver to Chester, boarding the vessel, and presenting Captain Ayres with the threat of an "American Exhibition."

We have only the patriots' unflattering description of the good captain—the "thick chunky Fellow" of the handbills—but presumably he was no fool and did not lack for courage. Few ship captains plying the dangerous Atlantic routes could afford to be cowards. But when the committee demanded that Ayres accompany them—leaving his ship, crew, and cargo of tea and other goods behind and bringing only the letters he carried with him from London—he realized he had no choice but to comply. Despite the threats contained in the handbills, he was treated courteously and must have breathed a sigh of relief upon seeing that the patriots carried no pots of tar or bags of feathers.

Ayres arrived in Philadelphia the next day and was lodged at William Bradford's London Coffee House. He quickly became something of a celebrity. Everywhere he went, he was followed by a crowd of curious onlookers; no one jostled or jeered at him, although a few small children offered up what Ayres later called "some small rudeness," which apparently included hurling pebbles at his shoes. Perhaps inspired by his guardians' politeness—

and despite seeing handbills calling for his tarring and feathering posted all over the city—Ayres attempted to fulfill his duty as the captain of a ship commissioned by the East India Company to transport cargo across the Atlantic. On December 27, he visited ex-consignee Thomas Wharton at Wharton's home, expressing that if he and the other consignees planned to refuse the tea, then he, Ayres, needed to register a formal protest. Wharton understood such formalities. He invited tea agent Jonathan Browne over, along with a notary, and waited until Captain Ayres officially asked him if he would accept the tea and pay the duty.

To which Wharton replied formally, as recorded by the notary: "While the tea belonging to the Honble East India Compy (under your Care) is subject to the Payment of a Duty in America we cannot Act in the Commission which they have been pleas'd to Honor Us with."

That same afternoon—December 27—Bradford and other patriot leaders escorted Ayres to Philadelphia's State House, the same building where, just a few years later, the Declaration of Independence would be signed (it is now known as Independence Hall). Constructed between 1732 and 1753, the large, handsome, red-brick building stood two and a half stories tall and served as the meeting place of the Pennsylvania general assembly. To the likely astonishment and dismay of Ayres, some eight thousand people had gathered, so many that the meeting had to be moved to the square outdoors. The crowd was Philadelphia's

PHILADELPHIA STATE HOUSE

largest to date, representing almost one-third of the city's population. Yet it was far more orderly than the Boston mobs that had convened at Old South Church. With Ayres showing a spirit of cooperation, no further mention was made of tarring and feathering, nor did anyone poke fun at his rotund stature. Instead, acting with "a Decorum and Order worthy [of] the Importance of the Cause," the meeting formed seven official resolves. Ayres would not be allowed to enter or report his cargo at the Custom's House, nor could he unload his tea. He would be allowed to stay in town until the next day—December 28—to provision for his return voyage. After doing so, he would proceed immediately to the *Polly*, which must then set sail with its cargo straight back to Great Britain. The resolves were clear: *Nothing* would be unloaded from the ship, neither tea nor anything else, including a brand-new carriage that James Wharton had ordered. The carriage (and all other items) would have to be reshipped later in vessels not besmirched with the taint of tea. To help Ayres on his way, Wharton and Browne would advance the good captain some money for reprovisioning before his trip back east.

Upon Ayres's acceptance of the resolutions, the eight thousand Philadelphians roared their approval. He left town the next day and was soon plying the stormy seas once again, bringing back to England the same tea he had left with. Lord Dartmouth, head of North American affairs for the British government, was much displeased upon hearing the news. He wrote to Pennsylvania governor John Penn, grandson of William Penn, and asked why he had sat by and done nothing about the situation. Penn replied that there was nothing he could have done; by the time he learned of the *Polly*'s arrival in America, the ship was already on its way back to England. Although that may have been true, Penn certainly could not have failed to notice one-third of the city's population clamoring about tea. Still, through a skillful combination of threats and politics, Philadelphia managed to rid itself of the largest consignment of tea the East India Company tried to foist on the colonies, showing that it was no longer England's metropolis, but America's.

CHAPTER FOUR

The Charleston Tea Parties

November 1773

and November 1774

"It would be criminal tamely to give up any of our essential rights as British subjects, and involve our posterity in a state little better than slavery."

The Charles Town Gazette

I f you were a young, well-to-do American male in the mid-1700s who liked to drink, carouse, and go crazy, then the place to be was Charles Town, South Carolina. The fourth largest colonial port, after Philadelphia, New York, and Boston, Charles Town was renowned for its plethora of taverns and inns, where—despite some of the fiercest antidrunkenness laws on the books—patrons drank wine, persimmon beer, rum "slings," "flips," and "toddies" while flirting with ladies of the night. A few of these ladies even ran their own pubs. One such bar owner, Elizabeth Carne, advertised that "Entertainment for Man and Horse" was on the menu at her Broad Street establishment, an intriguing inducement if ever there was one.

Charles Town (whose name gradually morphed into Charleston) was founded in 1670 by English settlers, many of whom had emigrated from Barbados. Initially, pirating was a favored occupation, but by 1700 residents realized that surer fortunes were to be made planting rice indigo and trading and owning slaves, a group who would soon make up half the city's population. Because of the prevalence of slave labor, a wealthy businessman could buy a huge amount of land and recoup the cost within three or four rice-growing seasons, provided he was smart enough to own (or share) a merchant vessel that could deliver his crops to England and other colonial cities.

If you were young and poor, however, Charleston was a wretched place to be. The city was filled with indigent whites seeking work (a side effect of a slave economy), and the vast legions of unemployed often turned to crime. The hot and humid lowland climate bred malarial mosquitoes, and the city was often struck by waves of epidemics. As the common saying went, Charleston was "in the Spring a paradise, in the summer a hell, and in the autumn a hospital." According to one British observer, who crafted this colorful poem, it was far from a comfortable place:

> Black and white all mixed together
> Inconstant, strange, unhealthful weather . . .
> Agues plenty without doubt
> Sores, boils, the prickling heat and gout
> Musquitoes on the skin make blotches
> Centipides and large cockroaches . . .
> Houses built on barren land
> No lamps or lights, but streets of sand.

THE CHARLESTON TEA PARTIES

The British weren't the only visitors shocked by the city's unpleasant aspects and decadent lifestyle. New Englanders on business were appalled by the constant bacchanal of eating and drinking. The sheer extravagance of the plantations, which often bore such ostentatious names as Vaucluse and Sans Souci, contrasted starkly with the puritan way of life. Worst of all was the way many plantation owners lolled around while slaves did all the backbreaking labor. Bostonian patriot Josiah Quincy, who visited Charleston in 1773, commented that "nothing I saw raised my conception of the mental abilities of this people." (Quincy kept his opinion to himself, however, since most planters were crack shots who also believed in the *code duello*.)

If there was one man who defied the stereotype of the rich, lazy plantation owner it was Christopher Gadsden—among the most underheralded patriots in American history. Born in Charleston in 1723 Gadsden inherited a large fortune from his father and became a successful import-export merchant. He traveled widely, fought alongside the British in both King George's War and the French and Indian War, became an elected member of the South Carolina general assembly in 1757, and began his long career as a gadfly against the mother country. Tall, stiff, and often cranky looking, he was the model of probity—perhaps in reaction to the excesses of his father, an inveterate gambler. Even his friends found him dogmatic and irascible, especially when he was roused to rage by the actions of the British Parliament. After watching him in the South Carolina assembly, Josiah Quincy remarked that Gadsden was "plain, blunt, hot, and incorrect, and very sensible. Meekness was not one of his Christian virtues."

Gadsden saw himself quite differently. He liked to say he was "Don Quixote the Second," a chivalrous romantic who jousted at windmills. One of the more famous legends about him involved a dispute with General Robert Howe. Gadsden thought the general was incompetent, and he shared this view with anyone who would listen. The general received word of these aspersions and challenged Gadsden to a duel. Ever the gentleman, Gadsden generously allowed Howe to "begin the ball play." Howe stepped off ten paces, leveled his .50 caliber dueling pistol, and fired, taking off a piece of Gadsden's ear, at which point Gadsden would have been within his rights to blow Howe out of his boots. Instead, he merely fired his pistol into the ground and declared his honor satisfied.

Gadsden was also actively involved with the local chapter of the Sons of Liberty. Charleston had protested the Stamp Act much as the other colonies had, by hanging the stamp collector in effigy and trashing his home, but the local Sons of Liberty went one step further. They organized a highly effective boycott of British goods, which soon began to pile up, unwanted, on the city's wharves. (Gadsden himself would patrol the harbor at night "to see if anything [was] moving among the shipping.") After the British repealed the Stamp Act and introduced the Townshend Acts, Gadsden led another, even more effective boycott, causing British imports to drop by 50 percent. The women of Charleston did their part by dressing in homespun and sporting homemade "liberty umbrellas." When the British repealed the duties in 1770, Gadsden was all for continuing the boycott, but, as in other colonies, the merchants hoped the British had learned their lesson, and they went right back to buying English goods.

Then, in the fall of 1773, the British dispatched seven ships full of underpriced East India Company tea across the ocean. The *London*, captained by Alexander Curling, carried 257 chests bound for Charleston. After an uneventful voyage, the vessel arrived in the harbor on December 1. Charleston was the second colonial port, after Boston, to receive one of the hated tea ships. Of course, local patriots knew the tea was coming. In late November, a pseudonymous writer in the *South-Carolina Gazette* had warned that the tea was a symbol of Parliament's determination to "raise a revenue, out of your pockets, *against your consent*, and to render assemblies of your representatives totally *useless*." A few days later, another patriot cautioned that Parliament would soon be taxing the colonists "for the very light of heaven." The day the tea arrived, handbills appeared all over town inviting residents to a meeting on December 3 in the Great Hall of the city's famous Old Exchange mercantile building. The meeting, organized by Christopher Gadsden and the Sons of Liberty was, as the *Gazette* stated, for people "who thought it would be criminal tamely to give up any of our essential rights as British subjects, and involve our posterity in a state little better than slavery."

Although those present elected wealthy landowner Gabriel Powell to serve as chairman, Gadsden essentially ran the show. He began with a complaint: Few merchants were present to show their solidarity. Obviously, a tea boycott would hurt business, but Gadsden would share in the pain; after all, he had made his fortune on imports and exports. The three tea consignees were summoned to the meeting and, upon arriving, soon agreed to refuse their shipments.

But that didn't completely solve the problem. Gadsden was concerned that the governor of South Carolina—who would receive the tea after the consignees refused it—would then bypass the middlemen and take the product directly to market. So Gadsden led a committee to seek out merchants and urge them to join the boycott. These local merchants offered a surprising amount of pushback. The majority agreed to accept no further shipments of tea (either from East India Company or from smugglers) in return for a provision allowing them, for the next six months, to continue selling the tea they already had on hand.

While Gadsden effectively closed off the market, the *London* and its 257 tea chests were still moored in Charleston Harbor. Captain Curling received several warnings to immediately weigh anchor or risk seeing his ship set ablaze. Similar letters threatening to burn both the ship and its cargo were received by the tea consignees as well as by captains whose vessels were anchored near the *London*.

After twenty-one days without payment of the duty on the *London*'s tea, Robert Dalway Haliday, the town's collector of customs, ordered the chests unloaded in the early morning darkness of December 22 and placed under lock and key in the basement of the Old Exchange building. Then, supplied with a new load of tea and a new captain, the *London* set sail for New York (where it would eventually play a role in another tea party; see page 107). The British were not entirely unhappy with this resolution. As Lord Dartmouth later commented, the Charleston Tea Party was "not equal in criminality to the proceedings in other Colonies."

But, a few weeks later, when Gadsden and the Sons of Liberty learned of the tea demonstrations in Boston and Philadelphia, they were incensed. They realized they were the only patriotic organization that had allowed tea to land in America; even worse, Charleston merchants were still selling the noxious weed, thanks to the six-month window they had negotiated.

Gadsden decided to lead a committee charged with weaning the population of Charleston, and that of South Carolina as a whole, from buying and drinking tea. His efforts were mostly futile: he made little headway with merchants (who were still enjoying healthy profits from tea sales) and had even less luck with housewives (who were now hoarding tea in case of future shortages). With considerable embarrassment, Gadsden wrote to Sam Adams in Boston that certain unnamed mercantile interests had thwarted the cause of liberty in his city.

Charleston's cause of liberty might have deteriorated even further had the British government not tried to retaliate against Adams and his local Sons of Liberty chapter. In the months after the Boston Tea Party, members of Parliament—and even King George himself—were eager to exact revenge on the rioting colonists. Lawmakers described the city as "a canker worm in the heart of America" and "a rotten limb which will inevitably destroy the whole body of that extensive country." One minister advised that "it would be best to blow the town of Boston about the ears of its inhabitants, and to destroy that nest of locusts."

Vengeance was delivered in the form of the Coercive Acts of 1774, which Americans quickly dubbed the Intolerable Acts. This legislation included the Boston Port Act, which effectively closed the city's harbor to all shipments until the East India Company had been reimbursed for losses caused by the tea destruction, and the Quartering Act, which required colonists to provide shelter to the British army. Sam Adams and the Sons of Liberty lost no time sharing the information and their indignation with the other colonies. Gadsden likely reveled in the news. Finally, here was an announcement that would motivate the people of Charleston to take action and support a boycott. The Intolerable Acts succeeded in making colonists realize, in the words of David Ramsey, one of the earliest historians of the American Revolution, that "the only favor the least culpable could expect was to be the last that would be devoured" by the British Crown.

Once again, Gadsden called for a nonimportation boycott (this time accompanied by a nonexportation agreement), but the measure was still too draconian for South Carolinians, and he had to be satisfied with heading the efforts to collect food for Boston, whose citizens were beginning to feel the pinch of the Port Act. Sending 194 whole barrels and 21 half-barrels of rice to Boston, Gadsden wrote to Adams: "We depend on your Firmness, and that you will not pay for an ounce of the damn'd Tea." By July, the residents of Charleston had at last come around to the idea of a nonimportation *and* a nonexportation agreement (although, with typical Charlestonian practicality, the latter would take effect only after the October rice crop shipment). Even though each of these actions was detrimental to his personal fortune, Gadsden never flinched. In his words, he would rather see his brand-new wharf destroyed—and himself "half cut to pieces"—than to submit to Great Britain. No longer would he refer to England as the "mother country," he told a friend. From now on, it was "our mother *in law*." (Gadsden would end up marrying three times.)

At last, it seemed, Gadsden's message was taking root. The

ranks of the local Sons of Liberty swelled, and several Loyalists found themselves covered in tar and feathers. In late June, the British ship *Magna Carta,* captained by Richard Maitland, arrived in Charleston Harbor. Maitland swore to the committee of patriots who greeted his vessel that, although he did have tea aboard, he had no intention of selling it and planned to return it to England. The mob didn't believe him. They jumped over the sides of the ship and threatened to tar and feather Maitland, who exited hurriedly via lifeboat and sought refuge aboard another British ship, the *Britannia*, which was lying off the coast. One observer wrote that "it is generally thought that if [Maitland] had fallen into their hands, it would have cost his Life." Once aboard the *Magna Carta*, the mob found one full chest and two half chests of tea, which were sent to the Old Exchange building to join the tea taken earlier from the *London*.

The *Britannia* eventually had its own day of reckoning. Some five months later, after a return visit to London, it arrived once again in Charleston Harbor in early November. Incredibly, the ship was loaded with seven chests of East India tea. According to an article in the *South-Carolina Gazette*, the ship's captain, Samuel Ball, "acknowledged having the mischievous Drug aboard" but declared "that he was an entire Stranger to [the tea] being on board his Ship, 'till he was ready to clear out, when he discovered that his Mate had received [the chests] in his Absence. . . . That, as soon as he made the Discovery, he did all in his Power to get them relanded, but all his Endeavours, for two Days together, proving ineffectual."

Ball took the added precaution of swearing under oath to a notary in London that the tea was not his, and he brought the notarized document with him, hoping that it would "acquit him from the Suspicion of having any Design to act contrary to the Sense of the People here, or the Voice of all America." The colonists decided to accept his story (even though it sounds wildly disingenuous) and instead turned their wrath on Robert Lindsay, Zephaniah Kinsley, and Robert Mackenzie, the merchants who had ordered the tea. The *Gazette* went on to tell the story of what happened next:

On Thursday at Noon, an Oblation was made to Neptune of the said seven chests of Tea, by Messrs. Lindsay, Kinsley and Mackenzie themselves; who going on board the Ship in the Stream, with their own Hands respectively stove the Chests belong to each, and emptied their Contents into the River, in the Presence of the Committee of Observation, who likewise went on board, and in View of the whole General Committee on the Shore besides numerous Concourse of People, who gave three hearty Cheers after the emptying of each Chest, and immediately after separated as if nothing had happened.

For good measure, the same issue of the *Gazette* recorded that a Charleston merchant who was found holding six chests of smuggled Bohea was forced to return them to the smuggler, along with a warning "to venture no more this Way." Charleston was finally serious about its tea boycott. As for Christopher Gadsden, he would go on to a distinguished career during the American Revolution. Before that, he was elected a South Carolina representative to the Continental Congress in Philadelphia in 1775 and developed a now-famous flag, known as the Gadsden flag, for the nascent U.S. Navy: it featured Benjamin Franklin's snarling rattlesnake set against a bright yellow background and the words "Don't Tread on Me" underneath. He eventually became a brigadier general and fought against the British during their successful attack on Charleston in 1780. After being taken prisoner and sent to Fort Augustine in Florida, Gadsen was confined to solitary for nearly a year because of his stubbornness in refusing to sign parole papers. He returned home a hero, refused to serve as governor because of declining health, and died in 1805.

CHAPTER FIVE

The New York Tea Party

April 1774

"What demon of discord blows the coals in that devoted province I know not!"

Prime minister Lord Chatham, after learning

of the New York riots

I n April 1774, the island of Manhattan was thirteen and a half miles long and, at its widest point, two and a half miles across (it's somewhat wider today because of landfill added over the centuries). Most of its 20,000 inhabitants were crammed into the mile or so area below present-day Chambers Street, and its avenues and alleys bustled with commerce.

The French and Indian War had been good to the people of New York City. Business prospered thanks to the city's deep and well-protected harbor, an ideal refuge for military and merchant vessels, as well as its natural waterway, the Hudson River, whence the British launched attacks into Canada.

During the war, the good burghers of New York provided thousands of pounds of bread to the British soldiers (albeit after raising the price 14 percent). Sugar, which New Yorkers imported from the West Indies and refined in Manhattan using the labor of slaves, was sold in hard-packed loaves. Gunpowder was produced by the thousands of barrels. British officers and enlisted men needed housing, and so hundreds of homes were built,

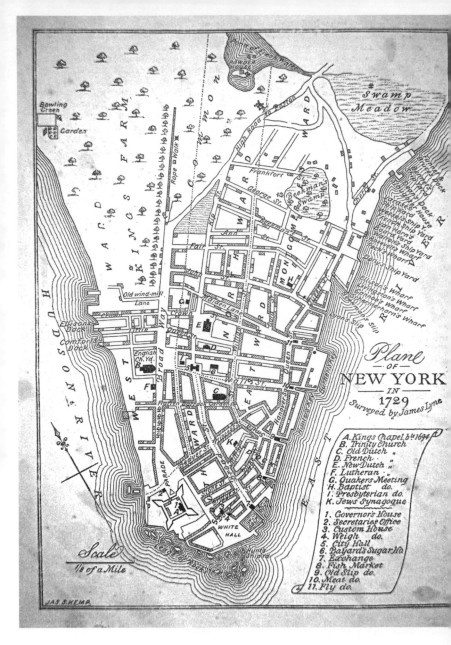

PLAN OF NEW YORK IN 1729

THE NEW YORK TEA PARTY

providing work for bricklayers, stonemasons, plasterers, and carpenters. New York soon became the colonial town with the most taverns (about 350 by war's end) and numerous rum distilleries. Tobacco also grew into a big business, with enterprising merchants packing snuff into animal bladders and selling them by the gross.

Clearly, New York had reaped more rewards from the French and Indian War than any other colony, but residents never displayed enough gratitude to satisfy English politicians. In 1764, when the British Parliament was debating the passage of the Stamp Act, former secretary of war Charles Townshend called Americans "children . . . planted by our care, nourished by our indulgence" and asked, "[w]ill they grudge to contribute their mite [a small copper coin] to relieve us from the heavy weight of the burden [of war debt] we lie under?"

Unfortunately for Townshend, New Yorkers were not exactly eager to lend a hand. Like many a war-swollen metropolis, the city collapsed into a major recession when the war revenue dried up. Adding insult to injury, the British now wanted to tax sugar, which New Yorkers used to produce rum, one of their primary exports. Even worse, residents were also being taxed in order to pay for the upkeep of garrisoned soldiers; the generous subsidies for the army's upkeep, which the British government had provided during the war, had since dried up.

Hit by tax after tax, New Yorkers began to organize into

boisterous protest groups, including, of course, their own chapter of the Sons of Liberty. The members of this group were generally artisans and self-made men, with little hint of aristocracy, and their ranks included Isaac Sears, John Lamb, and Alexander McDougall.

Nothing prepared the British for the vehemence of the New York protests. The colony was full of wealthy Loyalists who supported the Crown; if occasionally they disagreed with Parliament's actions, they would deliver a petition of protest, not an angry, shouting mob. Indeed, some two hundred New York merchants did sign an agreement stating they would accept no more goods from England while the Stamp Act taxes remained in place.

The impact of the Stamp Act was felt not just by wealthy merchants but also by the laboring classes—the carters, builders, seamen, tavern keepers, and street sweepers who were already hurting financially. A formal petition of protest was far too abstract a concept for them to support. On November 1, 1765, the day the Stamp Act took effect, a crowd of more than two thousand (described by onlookers as seamen, children, blacks, laborers, and "country people" from outside Manhattan) raged down to Fort George, at the southern end of the island. They carried an effigy of acting governor Cadwallader Colden, who was already hiding behind the walls of the fort, with its ramparts holding a hundred cannons loaded with grapeshot.

Although the colonies abounded with hated officials in the

lead-up to the revolution (Governor Thomas Hutchinson of Massachusetts jumps to mind), few were reviled more than seventy-seven-year-old Colden, described by one historian as "ornery, contrary and arrogant." The Sons of Liberty made it known throughout the city that the wealthy Colden had sought to enrich himself (and his son) through the Stamp Act. As a result, rioters felt no compunction about breaking into Colden's coach house, stealing his carriage and two of his sleighs, and—after carrying them through the streets in gleeful triumph—burning the items in front of the fort while the governor looked on. Next, the mob rampaged across the city to destroy the home of the major in charge of the British troops at Fort George; along the way, they consumed nine casks of the good officer's wine, stole his silverware, and smashed all the mirrors, windows, and china in the house. Anything they couldn't carry away they smeared with butter swiped from the pantry.

Well-to-do Loyalists were shocked by the violent display. Even though most New Yorkers agreed that Colden was, as one colonist described him, "extremely odious," Loyalists felt that the actions of the mob were unwarranted. Even patriot leaders, such as Isaac Sears, were concerned that the violence might career out of control. Back in England, the government was flummoxed. After learning of the riots, prime minister Lord Chatham thundered from the floor of Parliament: "What demon of discord blows the coals in that devoted province I know not!"

TEN TEA PARTIES

Little did Chatham realize that the demons were just beginning to wreak their havoc. Even after Parliament repealed the Stamp Act, New York mobs continued to clash with local British authorities. In one instance in May 1766, the Sons of Liberty erected a Liberty Pole in a public area in front of the barracks housing a British regiment. The provocation was clear: these tall wooden poles (usually surmounted with small flags or liberty caps, a kind of soft conical hat often seen in later depictions of the French Revolution) had become patriot symbols. Not surprisingly, the Sons of Liberty returned the next morning to discover their pole had been chopped to the ground. An angry mob assembled outside the barracks, and soon British soldiers with bayonets were battling New Yorkers armed with clubs and brickbats. The two sides beat each other bloody.

But that wasn't the worst of it. Three more times the Liberty Pole went up, three more times the redcoats tore it down, and three more riots ensued. One such clash, dubbed the Battle of Golden Hill, took place on what is today the Lower East Side, on a small hill that had once grown amber-colored grain. When the skirmish was over, British soldiers armed with bayonets and cutlasses had killed one colonist and badly wounded several others.

In 1770, after the repeal of the Townshend Acts, merchants sent employees brandishing quill and paper to the doorsteps of New Yorkers, who answered by a large majority that they wanted

New York governor Cadwallader Colden, one of the
most reviled leaders in the colonies

to resume trade and reestablish more cordial relations with Great Britain. Most New Yorkers opposed the kind of mob violence that had raged in their streets for the past five years, especially since it often spilled over into petty crime and muggings. The Sons of Liberty became, if not moribund, then at least quiescent for the better part of three years.

That is, until the Tea Act was passed.

By 1773 New York's economy still had not improved. Hundreds of people were crammed into the old municipal poorhouse, and crime was on the rise. So, when New Yorkers learned about the Tea Act—and the impending arrival of more than six hundred chests at their own port—they were ready to retaliate. One newspaper correspondent wrote: "It is hoped that Americans will convince [British prime minister] Lord North that they are not yet ready to wear the Yoke of Slavery and suffer it to be rivetted about their Necks, but that they will send back the Teas from whence they came."

Here, at last, was an issue the New York Sons of Liberty could rally around, and they did so with a vengeance. First order of business: sending messages to allies in other colonies, warning them of the danger, and then working to unite merchants, housewives, and tea smugglers in common cause against the East India Company. Radical patriot leader Alexander McDougall wrote a series of "Alarms," published in a patriotic journal, calling upon sea captains to "refuse the freight of the East India

Company's Tea." The Sons of Liberty discovered the identity of the New York merchants acting as company consignees—Henry White, Benjamin Booth, and Abraham Lott—and did their best to attack them, accusing each of being an "Enemy to his Country."

During the same week the Sons of Liberty held their first tea protest, omens and portents appeared through the city. A "considerable large whale" was spotted in the Hudson River (a rarity even then), which was followed by an earthquake, "preceded by violent rain, and immediately succeeded by very awful lightning and tremendous peals of thunder," that shattered china sets and fragile nerves in many a household. Bowing under considerable pressure, the three consignees issued a statement saying they would "decline receiving and selling" the tea. And with that news, New York governor William Tryon found himself grappling with the same question that had faced Governor Hutchinson in Massachusetts: When the tea finally arrived, what in the world was he supposed to do with it?

The Sons of Liberty were unsure what they planned to do, too. They looked initially to William Smith, a Loyalist (albeit a moderate one) and advisor to Governor Tryon, for advice on how to prevent the tea from landing. Smith was shocked to hear McDougall propose an extreme plan: "What if we prevent the landing and kill the Governor and all the Council?" The revolutionary fire had its spark, and, as Smith later recalled in his diary, "a new Flame is apparently kindling in America."

When Smith brought his concerns to Tryon, he found that the governor had already made up his mind. He told Smith he would allow the tea to land but refused to send the army to protect it. "I will use no Arms until after they have abused & disgraced their Govt. & themselves," Tryon said. "I will run the risk of Brick Batts and Dirt and I trust that you & others will stand by me."

On December 17, the day after the Boston Tea Party (although New Yorkers were as yet unaware of the event), the New York Sons of Liberty called for a huge meeting at town hall. Several thousand attendees listened as speakers read letters from Boston and Philadelphia expressing their solidarity with the people of New York. Next, the mayor, Whitehead Hicks, delivered a message from the governor. He told the crowd that Tryon agreed the tea should be returned to England, but first he would need to store it in Fort George until he received orders from Parliament allowing him to send it back. The crowd treated Hicks respectfully but disliked his decision, recognizing that it was, in effect, a trap: as soon as the tea left the ship, the hated threepence tax would have to be paid. The Sons of Liberty were left to wrestle over their next move. Would they accept the governor's proposal or consider an alternative?

Before a decision could be reached, Paul Revere came riding into the city with an electrifying story. Patriots in Boston had stormed aboard the tea ships and literally tossed the cargo overboard! Thomas Smith wrote that the news "astonished the Town," and tensions ran high as the New York Sons of Liberty made plans to host a tea party of their own.

But the winter dragged on without an appearance of the tea-toting *Nancy*, which had proven to be a hard-luck ship. En route to New York, it had been blown so far south by storms that it ended up in Antigua. In March, as it made its way up to New York, the *Nancy* met another storm, lost its anchor and a mast, and nearly capsized, with eighty Scots immigrants washed overboard to their deaths.

As the ship toiled through the frigid New England winter, a rather extraordinary deal was being brokered between the governor, the tea consignees, and the Sons of Liberty, showing that politics does indeed make strange bedfellows. Fearful of impending violence as well as of losing face with the colonists, Tryon arranged for Henry White, one of the consignees, to approach the Sons of Liberty and explain that Tryon would not try to land the tea, and the consignees would not accept the tea, if the Sons of Liberty would pay to have the *Nancy* reprovisioned before it headed back to England. The citizens of New York never learned of this secret deal; they knew only that the tea wouldn't land, and so they cheered the news.

On April 18, the *Nancy* finally arrived in Sandy Hook, New Jersey (a standard practice for many ships en route to the New York harbor). Immediately, the secret agreement was set in motion. Pilots refused to escort the ship or its captain, Benjamin Lockyer, any farther. Fifteen "husky" Sons of Liberty chained and padlocked the vessel's small boats in order to keep the crew from escaping into New York (some tried anyway, building a small raft and trying to float it over the side of the *Nancy*). The New York Sons of Liberty's moment in the sun had come, and they wasted no time taking advantage of it. On April 19, they distributed a handbill that read, in part:

To the Public.

The long expected TEA SHIP appeared last night at Sandy Hook, but the pilot would not bring up the Captain until the sense of the city was known. The committee [of Correspondence] was immediately notified of her arrival, and that the Captain solicits permission to come up to provide necessaries for his return. . . . Whenever he comes up, care will be taken that he does not enter the customhouse, and that no time be lost in dispatching him.

Continuing in the same vein two days later, the Sons of Liberty passed out another "To the Public" handbill, in which they summoned onlookers to wish bon voyage to Captain Lockyer as he departed New York for Sandy Hook and then on to Great Britain: "It is the desire of a number of citizens that he shall see with his own eyes their detestation of the measures pursued by the Ministry and the India Company to enslave this country."

The huge public meeting, scheduled for April 23, was designed to be a spectacular bit of propaganda for the Sons of Liberty—a way to demonstrate their influence without any risk of violence. It was a win-win situation for Loyalists and patriots alike, until something completely unexpected happened: *Another* tea ship, the *London,* showed up.

After unloading its cargo of tea in Charleston in December, the *London* had traveled up the coast under a different commander, one James Chambers. Chambers had a bit of a checkered history with New York. A longtime sea captain, he had delivered the first Stamp Act stamps to the city back in 1765. Now the Sons of Liberty received word (probably through contacts in Philadelphia) that Chambers was carrying eighteen chests of (probably smuggled) tea, which he planned to sell for his own personal profit.

When the *London* arrived at Sandy Hook, Chambers denied that he had any tea aboard and thus was allowed to continue on and dock at Murray's Wharf (at the foot of present-day Wall Street), which he reached about 4 p.m. on April 22. Once again, he was queried by citizens whether his ship carried tea, and he answered vehemently that it did not. But Chambers

COLONISTS ON THE RIVERFRONT OF NEW YORK CITY

had underestimated the temperature of the times, for the crowd was far too angry and persistent to be put off. Summoned by shouts and cries, hundreds of people poured aboard the *London* and began tearing apart the cargo. By this point, Chambers was confessing to anyone who would listen that, yes, he did have eighteen chests of tea on board, but the event had already descended into chaos. Some people smeared on war paints in homage to the Boston Mohawks; others hoisted up the tea chests, cracked them open, and dumped their contents overboard. In the confusion, Chambers decided wisely to make himself scarce.

The next morning, Saturday, April 23, was the day designated by New Yorkers to stage a demonstration to see Captain Lockyer off, along with the *Nancy*. A huge crowd—according to one newspaper, "the greatest number ever known in this city"—showed up at around 8 a.m. in front of the Coffee House on Wall Street, where Lockyer was lodging. A festive atmosphere reigned as the Sons of Liberty escorted the captain down to the wharf, where a pilot's boat awaited to take him back to his ship. A band played "God Save the King"—with a nice touch of irony—and church bells rang out all over the city. As Lockyer stepped onto the boat, a cannon at the base of the Liberty Pole—which had been erected once again, and this time sheathed in iron—fired a salute in honor of his departure.

The only thing that marred the circus atmosphere was the shouts of the mob as they tried to find James Chambers. "Where is he?" they cried. "Where did he go?" But Chambers was nowhere in sight. The Sons of Liberty would learn much later that Chambers had cut a secret deal of his own with Captain Lockyer, who agreed to let his fellow mariner stow away on his ship's return voyage to England.

The colonists never had any idea. They escorted Captain Lockyer back to Sandy Hook and sailed alongside the *Nancy* until it was six miles off the coast—resolutely headed for Great Britain—before turning around and steering back to the city in triumph.

To the Public.

THE long expected TEA SHIP arrived last night at Sandy-Hook, but the pilot would not bring up the Captain till the sense of the city was known. . The committee were immediately informed of her arrival, and that the Captain solicits for liberty to come up to provide necessaries for his return. The ship to remain at Sandy-Hook. The committee conceiving it to be the sense of the city that he should have such liberty, signified it to the Gentleman who is to supply him with provisions, and other necessaries. Advice of this was immediately dispatched to the Captain ; and whenever he comes up, care will be taken that he does not enter at the custom-house, and that no time be lost in dispatching him.

New-York, April 19, 1774.

PROCLAMATION INFORMING THE PUBLIC THAT A BRITISH TEA SHIP WAS PREVENTED FROM LANDING CARGO IN NEW YORK

CHAPTER SIX

The Chestertown
Tea Party

May 1774

"The act of the British parliament subjecting the colonies to a duty on tea, for the purpose of raising revenue in America, is unconstitutional, oppressive, and calculated to enslave the Americas."

From the Chestertown Resolves

C hestertown is a sleepy maritime center of some five thousand residents located on Maryland's Eastern Shore. The Chester River, a calm and wide tidewater stream, flows past its handsome, red-brick eighteenth-century houses and out into the reaches of the Chesapeake Bay. The *Chestertown Spy*, a local online newspaper, reports happenings under such old-timey headings as "Occurrences," "Disturbances," and "Fortnightly." In the summer, well-heeled vacationers arrive from Annapolis and Philadelphia to boat and swim and fish; in the winter, the town retreats into rainy quiet.

At one time each year—Memorial Day weekend—Chestertown explodes with visitors. The population swells by thousands. The town's quaint B and Bs are booked months in advance. There are wine tastings, a five-kilometer run/walk, a parade, and a garden show—typical Memorial Day fare, you might think, except for one unique addition: Men dressed up like colonial-era patriots storm aboard a replica of an eighteenth-century brigantine called the *Geddes* and throw chests of tea into the Chester River, all in honor of an event that took place on May 23, 1774—the Chestertown Tea Party.

Many of the cities whose stories are told in this book commemorate their tea parties with annual celebrations, but Chestertown's is the biggest party of them all. Its motto is "Often imitated, never equaled . . . since 1774," and there's truly nothing like it in any other state. *Everyone* dresses in colonial garb, from grandparents down to toddlers, and the ritual tossing-of-the-tea-into-the-river is usually accompanied by sailors from the *Geddes* splashing into the water. Such an energetic display is a bit odd in light of the ongoing mystery surrounding the event being commemorated, for some people think Chestertown's tea party never happened at all.

The village was founded in 1705 on the land of a former plantation along the Chester River. It offered a unique perk to skilled craftsmen, who were exempted from taxes for four years if they moved into the new town, which they soon did, and in large numbers. Designated as one of Maryland's Royal Ports of Entry, the waterfront settlement was one of only six places in the colony where ships could land and declare their goods for customs, thus making it an important port situated about halfway along the East Coast. Historian Adam Goodheart said it best when he described Chestertown as "a rest stop on the colonial I-95."

By the 1730s, Chestertown had become a thriving shipping hub. Its merchant-planters had stopped growing soil-exhausting tobacco and turned to wheat, a far more renewable crop; they began exporting grain and flour to the West Indies, Spain, the Azores, and Madeira on schooners built in local shipyards. These vessels returned laden with wine, fruit, and salt, in addition to their human cargo, slaves. Many planters became so rich after only four or five voyages that they were able to retire and build the sturdy brick houses along High Street, facing the Chester River, that still stand today.

The inhabitants of Chestertown were as sophisticated and well informed as any citizen of New York or Philadelphia, in part because of the influx of international vessels as well as the town's central location. Travelers originating in the south would take a ferry across the Chesapeake from Annapolis to Rock Hall and then continue overland by coach or horseback to Chestertown, where they usually stopped for a night's lodging before heading to Philadelphia and points north. Chestertown would be their stopping point on the return journey, too. In both directions, weary travelers would share news of the goings-on all across the colonies. In the years before the Revolutionary War, many famous people passed through Chestertown—George Washington and Thomas Jefferson, to name just two—and all commented favorably on the local taverns, or "ordinaries," as they were known. One notorious ordinary was Dougherty's, which sold "good West Indian rum, good cider and Madeira wine" and kept a female baboon chained in the courtyard for the edification of visitors. The taverns' courtyards were also where traveling acting troupes would present shows, their repertoire ranging from *A Midsummer Night's Dream* to *The Beggar's Opera*.

Despite the large population of old, wealthy, landed gentry, Chestertown was not generally a conservative town. The prominent families—the Smyths, the Ringgolds, the Wilmers—had fought with the British in the French and Indian War, but they later expressed outrage over the Stamp Act and the Townshend Acts, which they saw as attempts by the English monarchy to profit from the lucrative international trade upon which the town depended so heavily. In 1758, during the French and Indian War, the British quartered seven companies of redcoats in Chestertown over the winter; the locals resented their presence so much that a pitched battle broke out between them and the soldiers, ending with the death of a British sailor and murder charges filed against two young men from prominent families (both were convicted but later pardoned). This was a decade before similar tensions (namely, British troops quartered in a town that did not want them) led to the Boston Massacre.

Patriots in Chestertown were still deciding how to respond to the Tea Act of 1773 when, the following January, they heard the news of the Boston Tea Party. It wasn't long before a local chapter of the Sons of Liberty was formed by prominent young men like Thomas Smyth III, Thomas Ringgold V, and William

Carmichael; this last wore a self-designed ring bearing the Latin motto "*Manus haec inimica tyrannis*," or "This hand is the enemy of tyrants." Since no tea ships were immediately destined for Chestertown, there was nothing much for these patriots to do except exchange plenty of heated talk at Worrell's, the Sons' favored tavern.

But on May 13, Chestertown received word of the Intolerable Acts. The Sons of Liberty immediately gathered at Worrell's to vocally condemn Great Britain. They were upset not with the king (as is true of many colonists of the era, they still professed filial loyalty) but with his "corrupt and despotic ministry," meaning, Parliament and Lord North. Five days later, the Sons organized a public meeting at the Kent County courthouse. Attendees were presented with a statement that came to be known as the Chestertown Resolves:

> 1st — RESOLVED, that we acknowledge his majesty George III, King of Great Britain, France and Ireland, to be our rightful and lawful sovereign to whom we owe and promise all dutiful allegiance and submission.

> 2nd — RESOLVED, that no duty or taxes can constitutionally be opposed on us, but by our own consent given personally, or by our own representatives.

3rd — RESOLVED, that the act of the British parliament subjecting the colonies to a duty on tea, for the purpose of raising revenue in America, is unconstitutional, oppressive and calculated to enslave the Americas.

4th — RESOLVED, therefore, that whoever shall import, or in any way aid or assist in importing, or introducing from any part of Great Britain, or any other place whatsoever, into this town or country, any tea subject to the payment of a duty imposed by the aforesaid act of Parliament: or whoever shall willingly and knowingly sell, buy or consume, in any way assist with the sale, purchase or consumption of any tea imported as aforesaid subject to a duty, he or they, shall be stigmatized as enemies to the liberties of America.

5th — RESOLVED, that we will not only steadily adhere to the foregoing resolves, but will endeavor to excite our worthy neighbors to a like patriotic conduct, and to whoever, amongst, shall refuse his concurrence, or after complying, shall desert the cause, and knowingly deviate from the true spirit and meaning of these our resolutions, we will mark him

out as inimical to the liberties of America, an un-
worthy member of the community, and a person not
deserving our notice [or] regard.

6th — RESOLVED, that the foregoing resolves be
printed, that our brothers in other colonies may
know our sentiments as therein contained.

Signed by order of the Committee, W Wright, Clerk

These resolutions were fairly typical of the statements
being issued by Sons of Liberty chapters up and down the East
Coast. But a small addendum to the document suggests a hint of
the troubles to come:

N.B. The above resolves were entered into upon a
discovery of a late importation of dutiable tea (in the
brigantine *Geddes* of this port) for some of the neigh-
bouring counties. Further measures are in contem-
plation, in consequence of a late and very alarming
act of parliament.

Research by Adam Goodheart shows that the *Geddes* (a
local ship that may have been owned by Chestertown customs
inspector and merchant William Geddes) had arrived in port

from London on May 7. It was a brigantine, a smallish ship of about fifty tons, captained by John Harrison and manned by a crew of seven. The cargo was the property of thirty-seven-year-old merchant James Nicholson, who just happens to be one of the two young men pardoned in the killing of the British sailor in 1758. Nicholson was also a member in good standing of the town's Sons of Liberty.

According to customs records unearthed by Goodheart, a local inspector wrote on May 7 that the *Geddes* carried "European goods." But after (apparently) having second thoughts, the inspector went back and inserted the phrase "&EI" between the words *European* and *goods*. *EI* stood for East India, an indication that the ship could have been carrying anything from silk to tea.

Some scholars claim that the last sentence of the addendum is proof of the Chestertown Tea Party's occurrence. On May 13, as the story goes, the Sons of Liberty stormed out of Worrell's and marched down High Street in broad daylight. They boarded the *Geddes*, catching its crew unaware, and threw the chests of tea overboard, along with several sailors who resisted the assault. Crowds lining the Chester River cheered boisterously as both seaman and tea hit the water.

But the story has a few problems. For starters, no historical record of the event exists. In every other colonial tea-party location, patriot newspapers and committees of correspondence spread the news like wildfire. Note that, although the *Maryland*

THE CHESTERTOWN TEA PARTY

Gazette did publish the Chestertown Resolves, it made no mention of the tea party, nor do any known personal documents from the era, such as diaries or letters. In fact, the Chestertown tea party was never mentioned in a single book until 1899, when Fred Usilton wrote his *History of Chestertown: Gem City on the Chester*. Usilton was a notoriously unreliable historian who claimed that the Boston Tea Party took place on May 13, the day of the Chestertown Tea Party, when it in fact occurred some six months earlier.

In the 1950s, Usilton's son Fred revived the story for the 250th anniversary of the founding of Chestertown, and tourists embraced the tale. The first Chestertown Tea Festival, held in 1967, attracted 25,000 visitors. By that time, the date had been mysteriously changed to May 23, possibly to be closer to Memorial Day.

None of this means the Chestertown Tea Party didn't happen; it only suggests that no records survive, an unusual but not impossible turn of events. But further questions remain unanswered about the events (or lack thereof) that occurred in Chestertown on May 13, 1774. Chief among them is, where did the tea come from?

The *Geddes* was not one of the original tea ships that set sail from London, nor was William Geddes or James Nicholson an East India Company consignee. One of the most tantalizing theories suggests that Nicholson was certainly involved. Born in

The notorious James Nicholson, Chestertown merchant
and U.S. Navy commander

Chestertown in 1737, Nicholson grew up a member of a socially prominent family in one of the fine brick houses on High Street. His patriotic sentiments apparently ran so deep that the brawl with the British soldiers and sailors in 1758 resulted in him being charged with murder (although family connections got him off). After this incident, he enlisted in the Royal Navy and fought in the French and Indian War. Returning home around 1771, after time spent in New England, he became a merchant. Now with his patriotism very much on display, he joined the Sons of Liberty, signed the Chestertown Resolves, and was appointed by Thomas Smyth to be a member of the Committee of Correspondence.

Would such an ardent patiot *really* try to sneak the despised tea into his hometown? For further insights into Nicholson's character, we must skip ahead to the American Revolution, during which he didn't exactly distinguish himself. In October 1776, the Continental Congress appointed the first captains to the fledgling United States Navy, and Nicholson was at the top of the list, literally. He was named commander of the twenty-eight-gun frigate *Virginia*, one of the finest new ships in the Continental navy, and then spent the next two years coming up with excuses to avoid sailing his warship into Chesapeake Bay, which was patrolled by a British squadron. Finally, pressured by an impatient Congress, at the end of March 1778 he tried to slip past the British ships but ran aground on a sandbar. He then fled via the ship's boat, leaving his crew and vessel to be captured, without a shot being fired, by the Royal Navy. The next day Nicholson returned to the captured ship under a flag of truce to ask for his personal effects, although he later claimed he was trying (unsuccessfully) to get his men paroled. Upon hearing of this sorry affair, a fellow American officer wrote acerbically to a friend: "If the Devil were a coward I should think that he possessed some of our sea captains."

Despite it all, Nicholson had enough charm or personal connections or both to be appointed to pilot the barge that ferried George Washington across the Hudson River on his way to the first presidential inauguration in New York City, in 1789. Before his death in 1804, Nicholson was heavily involved in politics, becoming an ardent Republican and supporter of Thomas Jefferson (his daughter Hannah would marry Jefferson's secretary of the Treasury, Albert Gallatin). In 1795, Nicholson even challenged Federalist Alexander Hamilton to a duel, although (for reasons unknown) the contest never occurred.

In short, Nicholson had a history of changing his political stripes. He'd help kill a British sailor and then join the British navy. He'd ferry the Federalist George Washington across the Hudson and then challenge Washington's first Treasury secretary to a fight to the death. What was to keep him from smuggling tea for personal profit, despite his connections to the Chestertown Sons of Liberty? It's possible that outraged group members, having discovered that the tea on board the *Geddes* belonged to Nicholson, reacted explosively and spontaneously, storming down to the wharf to toss the tea into the river. Afterward, in a moment of clarity, they may have realized they'd exposed themselves to potential humiliation. What would happen if people learned that Nicholson—a member of their own in good standing—was a traitor for tea? And so perhaps they kept the affair hushed up. Instead of bragging about the tea destruction to the *Maryland Gazette*, maybe they promoted the Charlestown Resolves instead.

A less conspiratorial theory—and the one favored by Adam Goodheart—suggests the tea belonged not to Nicholson but to the captain of the vessel, John Harrison, who was attempting to smuggle a few chests on his own (without Nicholson's knowledge). Doing so was not unheard of, for captains loved to make a little money on the side. (Recall the tale of James Chambers aboard the *London* after the New York Tea Party, recounted on page 107.) In Goodheart's scenario, Nicholson is the hero—he discovered the tea, perhaps by dint of looking at the customs sheet or while unloading his own goods, and then informed his fellow Sons of Liberty. In righteous wrath, he followed them down to the *Geddes*, where the offending matter was thrown overboard. But if this was true, why did the patriots keep it confidential? It could be they felt no one would believe the truth. Perhaps Nicholson—and, by association, the Sons of Liberty—

might be perceived as "secret tories," agents for Parliament only pretending to be patriots.

Or maybe all of these theories are bunk. Maybe there was no tea party—maybe it was just a bogus legend engineered to boost tourism. Based on the historical record, I'm inclined to believe it did happen. It's likely there was tea aboard the *Geddes*, and equally likely that hot-blooded patriots would not have tolerated its presence for long. Alas, we may never know the truth. On May 24 the *Geddes*, loaded with a cargo of wheat and flour, sailed off for Madeira and into obscurity. No record exists of what happened to it afterward, just as there is no real record of what truly happened in Chestertown on May 13, 1774. Nevertheless, the Chestertown Tea Festival—as a celebration of what *might* and, even more important, *should* have happened—is a highly recommended way to spend a Memorial Day weekend.

CHAPTER SEVEN

The York
Tea Party

September 1774

"I find more persons here who call the destruction of tea mischief and wickedness than anywhere else."

John Adams, on the town of York, Maine

In June 1774, John Adams traveled to York, Maine, on a business trip. While there, he found himself at a dinner party seated next to Judge Jonathan Sayward, a prominent Tory and a representative of York at the Massachusetts general court. A crusty man in his early sixties, Sayward took it upon himself to lecture Adams about the country's current state of affairs. Adams was set to attend the first meeting of the Continental Congress in Philadelphia in September, prompting Sayward to say to him: "Mr. Adams, you are going to Congress and a great many things are in agitation. I recommend to you the doctrine of my former minister, Mr. Moody. Upon an occasion of some gloomy prospects for the country, he preached a sermon from this text: 'They know not what they do.'"

Adams took Sayward's "oracular jingle of words" in good grace, but privately he wrote to his wife, Abigail: "There is, in this town and country, a laodiceanism [indifference to politics] that I have not found in any other place. I find more persons

JOHN ADAMS

here who call the destruction of the tea mischief and wickedness than anywhere else." Adams would surely have been even more upset if he'd had access to Sayward's diary, in which the good jurist used the following language to document the Boston Tea Party:"The men of Belial arose in boston and took Possession of the 2 ships of tea and hoised all out and turned it into the Dock." To grasp the full import of these words, it helps to understand that Belial, a demon of antiquity, was one of the four crown princes of hell.

It was a tad overkill, perhaps, but then Maine always did have a strained relationship with the inhabitants of Boston. For starters, Maine was not considered a direct colony of Britain but rather a part of Massachusetts (it would not become a state until 1820). To some Mainers, it could feel like Massachusetts was wealthy Great Britain, and Maine her long-suffering and put-upon dependent.

Part of Maine's problem was that, for much of the 1600s and 1700s, it was isolated and thinly populated. Settlement moved forward in waves between five bloody Indian wars; each conflict left the Maine frontier deserted, sometimes for as long as twenty years, before homesteaders gradually moved northward again. It was a tough place to eke out a living. People subsisted by farming, fishing, and lumbering, and sometimes a combination of all three, but only a few lucky merchants and landowners grew wealthy.

Winters were hard, and starvation was a real possibility. Often the only thing saving the countryside from famine was the arrival (weather permitting) of foodstuffs at Maine's chief port of Falmouth. Most Mainers preferred rum over tea, since the former was cheap, abundant, and soothing, warming one's insides during the northeast's frigid winters (it was also a nice way to forget about those grinding twelve-hour workdays). Twentieth-century Maine writer Kenneth Roberts dug up an authentic colonial recipe for hot buttered rum—made with butter, boiling water, and cinnamon—but a popular variation substituted hard cider for the water, resulting in a concoction that, as Roberts says, should be treated "like a high explosive." He claimed that one could drink cider-based hot buttered rum in December and not wake up until May, which was probably the point.

In many frontier taverns, Mainers raised toasts to King George but not to the wealthy inhabitants of Boston—merchants like Thomas and John Hancock, Nathan Philips, Ichabod Jones, and Nathaniel Kent—who had advanced the credit on which these farmers, small businessmen, and fishermen lived. But, to be fair, in return their merchant counterparts served as the vital market for Maine's many loads of hay, lumber, and cod, in much the same way that the Great Britain of an earlier colonial era had provided the capital to fund the founding of America.

When the Sugar Act and Stamp Act were announced in Maine, political unrest quickly followed. These laws placed a

Mainers put in grueling twelve-hour workdays—
no wonder they indulged in a little rum.

premium on goods (hot buttered rum included) that Mainers needed even more than other colonists. Rowdy protestors attacked the customs inspectors and provincial officials who had agreed to oversee the distribution of the stamps. In 1766, a mob grabbed a smuggled shipment of sugar and rum belonging to a Falmouth merchant literally from behind the backs of customs inspectors, who had stored the products in a warehouse and were supposed to be guarding the building. Such mob seizures of confiscated smuggled goods were known locally as "rescues"; as Francis Bernard, then the governor of Massachusetts, reported to the Crown: "Formerly a rescue was an Accidental or occasional Affair; now it is the natural and certain Consequences of a seizure, and the Effect of a predetermined Resolution that the Laws of Trade shall not be executed."

But the mobs didn't always target representatives of the British government. Sometimes, a well-to-do merchant was confronted by an angry group of thugs simply because he was well-to-do. Possibly the most violent attack took place in the town of Scarborough and involved a rich store owner named Richard King. Those who owed King money falsely claimed he supported the Stamp Act; this lie gave the mob a convenient excuse to attack his house, which they did in a frenzy in March 1766. The troublemakers tore out interior paneling, threw furniture through windows, and stole his account books. They left a note claiming they were "Suns of luberty," but in fact they were mainly thugs out to destroy a wealthy man just because he was wealthy. The unfortunate King became a favorite whipping boy of these types of criminals before his death, in 1775—mobs beat him, smeared human waste on his home, and at one point forced him to kneel publicly at gunpoint and pledge allegiance to the patriot cause.

At least three Mainers attended the Boston Tea Party at Griffin's Wharf: Benjamin Burton, a seventeen-year-old brick-layer's apprentice from York named Benjamin Simpson, and Captain James Watson. While Burton was in the hold of one of the ships, helping to operate the sling that lifted the heavy chests, Watson was on deck helping to break open the tea chests (and filling his pockets with loose leaves, apparently unobserved by his more doctrinaire Bostonian compatriots). As Paul Revere galloped away to deliver the news of the event to the south, these three men brought it back to their individual communities, and word spread throughout the colony. Many Maine towns reacted happily, others fearfully. For its part, Simpson's hometown of York steered a middle course, voting to thank the town of Boston "so far as they have Constitutionally exerted themselves in support of their Just liberties and privileges."

This measured response was the result of influence of Judge Jonathan Sayward, whose Loyalist leanings hadn't been altered by the events of the past decade. As a representative to the Massachusetts general court, Sayward was one of seventeen members who voted in 1768 to retract an inflammatory letter the patriots had sent to Governor Bernard protesting the Townshend Acts. Ninety-two others voted in favor, and the letter stood. These men were praised as heroes, with Paul Revere casting a silver punch bowl inscribed to "The Immortal 92." Revere also produced a cartoon castigating Sayward and the other "Rescinders," the lot of whom were shown being sent to hell. In the drawing, Revere singled out Sayward as "the Chief Sooth-Sayer and Grand Oracle of Infallibility," meaning that he pompously forecast all types of disasters that would occur if the colonists stood up for their rights. A worried Sayward wrote in his diary: "Disorder have Infused and the 17 are treated with all Contempt and the printers are full against us." Although York saw fit not to reelect Sayward to the general court, the judge retained a lot of influence there. John Adams wrote, in the same letter to his wife mentioned above, that Sayward "insinuates sentiments and principles into people in a very subtle manner; a manner so plausible that they scarcely know how they came by them." Coming from a master propagandist like Adams, that is a true compliment.

In the wake of the Boston Tea Party, increasing numbers of Maine settlements were turning radical. Falmouth voted to ban the selling and drinking of tea in town, but since its merchants had 2,500 pounds of the stuff on hand—a heavy investment— they were not considered trustworthy enough to keep the resolve. A handbill soon appeared, produced by the local

Committee for Tarring and Feathering, declaring that no one in town should doubt what would happen to those who bought or consumed tea. The notice was signed: "Thomas Tarbucket, Peter Pitch, Abraham Wildfowl, David Plaister, Benjamin Brush, Oliver Scarecrow, and Henry Hand-Cart." Falmouth merchants got the idea and stopped selling tea.

In April, the British Parliament passed the Boston Port Acts in revenge for the destruction of the tea in that city's harbor. It was a financial disaster for Maine, since trade with Boston was residents' primary source of revenue. Yet, when patriots in Boston faced penury and starvation, Maine responded by sending firewood and fish and potatoes, everything they had, in still another demonstration of growing unity against the British. In general elections held in York in June, patriots swept the slate, causing Sayward to fume to his journal that the freshly elected were "madmen and hotheads." Under the new leadership, York voted to boycott tea.

Then, in September 1774, a shipload of tea arrived. As Judge Sayward described the incident on September 28:

> The last week was a week of Confusion in town. Capt. James Donnell from Newfoundland brought in a small quantity of tea at which a number were uneasy and chose a committee who took it out of the Vessel of Donnell and locked it in a store of Capt. Grow.

TEN TEA PARTIES

James Donnell was Sayward's nephew and captain of the sloop *Cynthia*. When Donnell docked at Keatings Wharf in York on September 15, he was carrying 150 pounds of tea that Sayward had ordered from British Canada. On the face of it, this act was sheer madness. Why would Sayward provoke the York patriots in this fashion? Did he really think he could import the most hated commodity in the colonies without upsetting his fellow citizens?

If he did, he was sadly mistaken. Local patriots formed a committee that agreed to transport the tea to a safe place (the basement of Edward Grow's store, which was about a block from Sayward's home) "until further Discovery could be made." The next night, the patriotic paper, the *New Hampshire Gazette* wrote, "a Number of Pickwacket Indians came into Town and broke open said Store and carried [the tea] off: which has not been heard of since." None of those charged with "guarding" the tea gave the raiders any trouble, and if any townspeople saw York's "invisible" tea party, they remained silent about it for posterity.

Sayward claimed he didn't know who took the tea, or who returned it, but that seems unlikely. In a town as small as York, he must have had an idea who the culprits were. It's possible that Sayward and the patriots worked out a deal—a way, as historian James S. Leamon has claimed, for York to "destroy its tea publicly while drinking it privately—a painless sort of radicalism." Or perhaps the patriots simply stole the tea and returned it as a warning.

Sadly, the theft of the tea was just the first of many more

unlucky incidents to befall Jonathan Sayward. He was constantly targeted because of his wealth, his Loyalist views, or both. On October 25, he recorded in his faithful diary: "I am informed I am to be mob'd this day." When he tried to preside over his courtroom, patriots burst in and gave impassioned speeches, causing uproars. In late spring of 1775, after the battles of Lexington and Concord, Sayward was called before a town meeting because, as civic records indicated, "the Town [was] somewhat uneasy and disaffected with the conduct of Jonathan Sayward Esq., supposing him to be not hearty and free for the Support & Defence of our Rights, Liberties & Privileges in this Dark & Difficult Day, but rather the contrary."

Apparently, Sayward attended and made a speech of his own, which the town committee found "satisfactory." Still, by the end of the year, he was exhausted, as his final diary entry in December shows:

> I am now arrived to the close of the year through the forbearance of God it had been a year of Extraordinary trials: besides the Death of my wife (the greatest of all) . . . on the 12 Sept. I have lost a new Sloop . . . and . . . one or more cargoes from the West Indies . . . but this is but small Compared with the Hazzards I have and am still in on account of my political sentiments and Conduct.

Sayward was harangued on the street by strangers. He was slighted by former friends. All his judicial offices were taken away. He lived, he said, "in Constant Danger of being Driven from my Habbitation so that that I have constantly kept £200 Lawfull in Gold and paper currency in my Pocket for fear of Sudainly being removed from my Abode." The town committee read his correspondence, and he was forced to swear that he had no treasonous inclinations.

Sayward's wealth remained intact, and he probably could have made arrangements to flee to British Canada or even to the Penobscot Peninsula (occupied by the British during the war), but instead he stubbornly insisted on staying in Maine. He spent his final years in the company of his granddaughter Sally Wood, who would become America's first female gothic novelist. Together they entertained the likes of John Hancock and, yes, John Adams at their home in York. He died in 1797, at the age of eighty-four.

Adams, who was elected U.S. president the year Sayward died, told people he thought the old Tory was the most courageous Loyalist he'd ever met.

CHAPTER EIGHT

The Annapolis
Tea Party

October 1774

"We will commit to flames or otherwise destroy as the people may choose, the detestable article which has been the cause of our misconduct."

Tea consignees James Williams, Joseph Williams, and Anthony Stewart

In the decade prior to the American Revolution, "Annapolis ... was the most famous, highly cultivated and superlatively gayest city of the American Plantations." Or so wrote Elihu Samuel Riley, a quirky nineteenth-century social historian who chronicled a century's worth of goings-on in this maritime city on Maryland's historic coast. According to Riley, Annapolis had earned the reputation of being both the "Athens of America" (because of its wise lawyers) and the "Paris of America" (because of its beautiful women). Charles Carroll, the wealthiest man in eighteenth-century America (net worth £2 million), lived there, as did a good hundred or so "haughty aristocrats" who, in Riley's words, "sat on carved chairs, at curious tables, amid piles of ancestral silverware, and drank punch out of vast, costly bowls from Japan, or sipped Madeira half century old." A thousand lesser luminaries inhabited sturdy, two-story brick houses in a city that had been designed, in 1708, after the great capitals of Europe, with cobblestone streets radiating from a center circle that contained the capitol building. Gambling, horseracing, and drinking in the city's dozens of taverns helped the gentle people of Annapolis deal with what Riley nicely calls "the ennui of the moment."

Maryland was unique in British North America for its stature as the last remaining proprietary colony of the Crown. In the early days of English settlement in America, the ruling monarch granted large land tracts to a single individual or proprietor (such as William Penn of Pennsylvania), who would then administer it under a royal charter. However, as more and more colonies were created, British rulers increasingly wanted direct control (and the revenues it provided); thus nearly all the proprietary colonies were converted to so-called Crown colonies run by officials appointed by the king. The lone exception was Maryland, which retained proprietary rule under the Calvert family. This arrangement generated a small fortune for the Calvert family, as much as £10,000 in taxes and rent every month (approximately $1 million a month in today's currency). And those taxes were in addition to all the new fees (like the Townshend Acts) imposed by Parliament on the colonies as a whole.

In the years before the Revolutionary War, the wealthy merchants and landowners who held power in Maryland were divided into two factions, one conservative and the other radical, that engaged in a bitter power struggle to decide the best way of responding to repressive British policy. The conservatives—men like Samuel Chase and Charles Carroll—advocated a peaceful protest against Britain through the use of petitions and diplomacy. The radical faction, spearheaded by John Hall and Matthias Hammond, recommended mob action instead. It was these wealthy radicals who organized the mob that, carrying sacks of feathers and pushing wooden carts with tar barrels, chased stamp collector Ebenezer Hood from Annapolis in 1765.

The hapless protagonist who became the pivot point in this power struggle was a man named Anthony Stewart. Born in Scotland in 1738, Stewart had immigrated to the colony of Maryland in 1753 and established himself as a successful merchant. In the mid-1760s, he married Peggy Dick, daughter of well-to-do importer James Dick. Stewart's father-in-law took him into the firm, and by 1770 Dick & Stewart had become the most successful import-export concern in Maryland, sending tobacco and cloth to England in return for such commodities as paper and tea. Stewart occupied a beautiful home with Peggy (the house still stands today on Hanover Street in Annapolis) and settled down to a life-plan that, presumably, did not include tarring and feathering, hanging in effigy, or civil upheaval.

But, in 1770, James Dick and Anthony Stewart found their Annapolis business disrupted when the Association of Anne Arundel County, a committee run by wealthy patriots of the area, declared a boycott of all British goods upon which taxes had been placed under the Townshend Acts. The association also

functioned as the town's Committee of Correspondence, helping to spread the news of British outrages to other colonies.

Shortly after the boycott was established, the brig *Good In-
tent* arrived from London with a load of merchandise ordered
by Dick & Stewart and other local merchants. The association refused to allow the ship to unload any of the goods onboard the
ship, even those not subject to the Townshend taxes. Eventually,
a dismayed Stewart and his father-in-law were forced to send
the vessel back to England, unloaded, and thus at great financial
loss. (Ironically, the British repealed the Townshend Acts even as
the ship headed back to London.) Amid the confusing array of
protests and patriotism that characterized the years leading up
to the revolution, the two merchants would disagree over the
best way to act. When in 1773, after passage of the Tea Act, the
association demanded that all merchants sign an agreement refusing to bring tea into America, Dick, elderly and easily intim-
idated, put his name to the paper. Stewart refused.

After the Intolerable Acts were passed in April 1774, the association met again in Annapolis and declared that, until the laws
were repealed, lawyers were prohibited from bringing suit against
any citizen who owed money to Great Britain. This was a boon
to numerous, heavily indebted merchants in Annapolis at a time
when being in arrears could mean lengthy prison sentences
under horrible conditions; it also demonstrates how these
protests were often married to commerce. This marriage was fur-

ther underscored when the association met with representatives of every county in Maryland and decided to continue the boycott on tea and other British goods but tabled a proposal to ban the export of tobacco to England until the current crop was harvested and sold.

Tensions in Annapolis reached the boiling point with the arrival of the brig *Peggy Stewart*. Owned by Dick & Stewart, the ship was named after Dick's daughter and Stewart's wife and was used to transport cargo between London and Annapolis; other merchants were also permitted to lease space on board. It had docked in London in February 1774, carrying a load of tobacco owned by a rival Annapolis firm named Wallace, Davidson & Johnson. After the cargo was unloaded, Richard Jackson, the ship's captain, had instructions from Stewart to try to sell the old brigantine, which was in need of almost constant repair. If he failed to find a buyer, he was to load it with the best available cargo and return to Annapolis. Unable to convince any takers, Jackson loaded the *Peggy Stewart* with fifty-three indentured servants, whose passage would be paid by the masters receiving them. With additional room still remaining on board, Jackson looked around for more cargo.

Enter Thomas Williams, the London representative of a firm run by his brothers Joseph and James, and a rival of Dick & Stewart. Williams asked Jackson to deliver to Annapolis 2,320 pounds of Bohea. It's unclear why Jackson accepted a cargo he knew would be embargoed; some historians believe he was hoping to smuggle the tea into the country. But the most commonly accepted theory is that Jackson was duped, and Williams, hoping to ruin his rival Stewart, had unloaded the tea onto the unsuspecting captain by pretending it was a cargo of linen. To avoid the possibility of being charged with smuggling, Williams accurately declared the tea on the British customs manifest but concealed the true contents from Jackson, who didn't discover what the shipment contained until he was already at sea, in bad weather, and with no choice but to continue on to America. This narrative is supported by a letter written by Williams to a counterpart in the firm of Wallace, Davidson & Johnson while the *Peggy Stewart* was en route, which hints that: "I should not be surprised to hear that you have made a Bon Fire of the *Peggy Stewart*."

When the ship did arrive in Annapolis on October 14, Anthony Stewart as well as Joseph and James Williams expressed astonishment upon discovering its cargo of tea. Disavowing responsibility, the Williams brothers refused to pay the duty, which was necessary to allow it—and everything else on board—into the port. But when Stewart walked down to the wharf to inspect his ship, he discovered the cargo of indentured servants, which, according to Maryland law, also had to remain aboard until all import taxes were paid. Stewart knew that if he didn't pay the duty on the tea within twenty days, the people aboard would be sentenced to a journey back to London through autumnal storms on a leaky vessel, a journey many of them were unlikely to survive.

Thus, to get the servants ashore, Stewart paid the duty. He left the Bohea on board, hoping that by doing so he would appease radical elements in the association. But his troubles were only beginning.

In further efforts to avert a disaster, Stewart and the Williams brothers sent a letter to the association, which read, in part:

> This is to inform you that the brig *Peggy Stewart* is just arrived from London ... and has got many goods on board for us, among which are a few chests of tea. Although agreeable to our order, yet it is contrary to our expectation, as we was in great hopes that the tea would not have been shipped. But as it have unlucky come to hand, and as the sale of it is disagreeable to our friends and neighbors, we are, therefore, willing to leave to your determination what is to be done with the said tea, and will readily acquiesce in any measures you may suggest, either in landing it or storing it, or reshipping to London or West Indies or elsewhere.

Admittedly, this document is fairly weasel-y. The tea was "agreeable" to their order, yet they had hoped it would not be shipped? In addition, 2,320 pounds of tea was more than "a few chests." Captain Jackson added to the letter a sworn affidavit stating that the tea had been placed on the ship without his knowledge, and the association seemed to accept this as truth. Which left Stewart and the Williams brothers to shoulder the blame.

Prior to a planned association meeting on October 19, Stewart approached Charles Carroll, the group's leader and one of its most conservative members, and reiterated that he was willing to dispose of the tea any way the group chose. After pondering the proposal for a moment, the judicious Carroll—a future signer of the Declaration of Independence—suggested that Stewart state his willingness to publicly burn the tea as well as write a letter explaining just why he had paid the duty (the act deemed most offensive by the association). The letter, published in the *Maryland Gazette* on October 16, stated that Captain Jackson had told Stewart that the vessel was "very leaky." Upon discovering that the "53 souls on board" would be sent back to England if he did not pay duty on the tea, Stewart thought that "both humanity and prudence" dictated he should pony up and release the human cargo. He reiterated once again that he was happy with whatever the association wanted to do with the tea, including the decision to burn it.

The group met in a full public meeting on Wednesday morning, October 19, to consider what had occurred and to review Stewart's proposal. Almost immediately, Stewart and the

THE ANNAPOLIS TEA PARTY

Williams brothers discovered that the association was not inclined to be lenient. Radical members rewrote the letter in more humiliating terms, which Stewart and the Williams brothers were forced to sign and read aloud to the assembled: "We, James Williams, Joseph Williams and Anthony Stewart, do severally acknowledge that we have committed a most daring insult and act of the most pernicious tendency to the liberties of America . . . we [promise] we will commit to flames or otherwise destroy as the people may choose, the detestable article which has been the cause of our misconduct."

The embarrassment was too much to bear. The Williamses broke from Stewart, claiming to all who would listen that "we are most cruelly made liable to the same degree of censure as Mr. Stewart, who paid the duty." They also complained about the trauma of being forced to read the letter "in the midst of an incensed people," who were reportedly calling for them to be hung. These protests must have been effective, for as the day wore on, and more and more people began spilling into the meeting from local taverns and meeting halls, public indignation shifted onto Stewart. Cries arose that he should be made "to wear a suit of tar and feathers," a punishment particularly worrisome to Stewart, whose wife was about to give birth to their first child.

In his 1887 book *The Ancient City: A History of Annapolis, in Maryland*, Elihu Riley wonders "just when the [association's] actions ended and the people's began." In other words, how did the disagreement boil over into mob violence? Records suggest that a radical patriot named Matthias Hammond likely played a role. Hammond had already seized upon the incident to further inflame sentiment against Great Britain, claiming that to accept even the most abject of apologies from Stewart was not in the interests of radicals. What was important was that "the wicked Mr. Stewart," as Hammond wrote in a series of handbills, be made to stand in for the king of England. These documents are interesting, because, as Stewart later complained, Hammond omitted to mention the role of the Williams brothers in the affair and conveniently forgot to state that all three men had voluntarily brought the matter of the tea to the association's attention. In his haste to whip up popular opinion against one man, Hammond also neglected the matter of the many others whose fates hung in the balance—the indentured servants—which goes a long way toward explaining Stewart's decision.

Stewart left the October 19 meeting after agreeing (along with the Williamses) to burn the tea with his own hands. The association had voted on a measure to burn the *Peggy Stewart* as well, but the conservative majority voted it down. Likely believing his ordeal was nearly at an end, Stewart had good reason to hurry home: he had received an urgent message that his wife was in childbirth.

Upon reaching his house, however, he discovered yet another crisis on his doorstep. Hammond and a firebrand physician and businessman named Dr. Charles Alexander Warfield had organized a mob at the home, which fronted the harbor. As Stewart paced the second floor, occasionally glancing out the windows, Warfield encouraged the crowd to construct a miniature gallows. Shouting up the stairs, Warfield demanded that Stewart destroy his ship and build another, to be named *James Wilkes*, after a liberal member of Parliament who supported the American cause.

An elderly James Dick tottered downstairs and begged the mob to disperse, but the group refused to listen. Fearful for the lives of his daughter and his family, he agreed to burn the ship. At this point, Stewart also surrendered, ventured downstairs, and promised to burn his vessel. He and the Williams brothers were led down to the harbor; by this time, according to Riley, Stewart needed to be accompanied by "several gentleman to protect him from personal violence." The three men were taken aboard. With sails set and colors flying, the ship was deliberately run aground at a point that is today part of the grounds of the U.S. Naval Academy. The ship was led to that spot, Riley claims, "in order that Mrs. Stewart, the invalid [childbearing] wife of the owner of the vessel, could see the conflagration from the window of her residence." With the mob jeering and shouting, Stewart applied a torch to the vessel and, in a matter of a few hours, the *Peggy Stewart* and "the obnoxious tea" were ashes.

As with almost every incident of tea destruction that occurred in the colonies, as with the American Revolution itself, the violent edges of the Annapolis Tea Party have been tempered by the passage of time and the erasure of memory. Anthony Stewart might have been framed and unjustly pilloried by businessmen out to ruin him. His aging father was terrified, and his wife was likely traumatized during childbirth. But it was all in the name of a revolution of which Stewart was on the losing side. He and his family would later flee Annapolis to the protection of New York and then to Nova Scotia, where he helped found a community of British Loyalists that is now New Edinburgh. Although Stewart managed to hang on to much of his fortune, Annapolis continued to be a cursed city for him. During a visit there in 1791, he died of a heart attack.

In 1904, the Annapolis Tea Party was commemorated with a heroic mural called "The Burning of the *Peggy Stewart*," which still exists on the west wall of the Criminal Court Lobby in the Clarence M. Mitchell Jr. Courthouse. In 1974, the Tea Party Bicentennial created a silver ingot honoring the revolutionary heroes who set fire to the ship. There is even a Peggy Stewart tea offered by Eastern Shore Tea Co., which is served at the yearly commemoration of the event; according to the packaging, its taste is "reminiscently smoky," to recall the burning of the old ship and its "detestable weed." But probably the most permanent reminder of the event is the copper marker affixed to the outer wall of a residence hall on the grounds of the U.S. Naval Academy, which reads:

THE ANNAPOLIS TEA PARTY

Near this spot which was then the shore of the bay,
the Brig **"Peggy Stewart"** was burned by her
owner, **"Anthony Stewart,"** October 19, 1774.
To pacify the indignation of the
citizens roused by the payment of
duties on seventeen boxes of tea
imported in the brig.

CHAPTER NINE

The Edenton and Wilmington Tea Parties

October 1774

and March 1775

"Maybe it has only been men who have protested the king up to now. That only means we women have taken too long to let our voice be heard."

Penelope Barker, hostess of the Edenton Tea Party

We hear from Westchester, that last week one of the inhabitants receiving a Curtain Lecture from his wife, he wish'd her Tongue was cut out; whereupon the good obedient Woman snatched up a Razor, and immediately cut off [a] great Part of that unruly Member, and had not the great Effusion of Blood put her life in danger, doubtless it would hereafter be found a grateful, as well as unprecedented Sacrifice. Happy Man! How rare a thing is it to find a Wife so good-natured and obliging in these Parts!

—The *Boston Evening-Post*, October 8, 1750

A *curtain lecture* is an archaic term for a marital scolding, so called because it occurred within the confines of a curtained bed. But clearly the incident described above was no ordinary husband-and-wife quarrel. Did the woman really cut off her own tongue? In bed? As penance for telling her husband to remove his muddy boots before entering the living room? Or was it done out of furious, self-destructive anger at her lot in life?

It's hard to know if this mid-eighteenth-century article from a prominent Boston newspaper can be taken at face value—one hopes it's simply an attempt at humorous hyperbole—but the writer's gleeful tone is irrefutable and speaks volumes about the life of women in the American colonies. In most households, women were expected to stay home, bear children (on average, about one child every two and a half years, with breastfeeding effectively acting as birth control), and raise their offspring hearthside. Engaging in other activities could be viewed as suspicious. The stereotype of Protestant Christians unwilling to forgive women for cozying up with the serpent in the Garden of Eden can be heard in the words of New England preacher Cotton Mather, who wrote: "[A] woman had the Disgrace to go first in that horrid and woeful Transgression of our first Parents."

Colonial men both feared and loved the opposite sex, in equal measure, and never more so than in the mid- to late 1700s, when women began expressing themselves in the burgeoning new marketplace provided by the flood of British manufactured goods into the American colonies. They began dressing with style and color. Even worse, as one male newspaper essayist commented bitterly, "it is the ambition of the ladies to appear handsome *in their eyes only*," that is, without consideration of the opinions of men.

These "new, bolder women," as historian T. H. Breen calls them, also drank tea. In fact, they seemed to guzzle the stuff all day, prompting one Swedish scientist visiting America to speculate that the staining effect of the dark liquid was the cause of their unusually discolored teeth. Men drank their fair share of the brew, too—one woman wrote that the gentlemen she knew were as "great *Tea-Sots* as any of us"—but women turned the consumption of tea into a private ritual, and their afternoon parties were closed to men. They alone knew the secrets of "the Ceremony of the Tea Table" and the ritualized use of "Cups, Saucers, Slop-Basin, etc."

Here, at last, was an opportunity for women to enjoy a small measure of freedom, a fact that made some men nervous. Who knew what they gossiped about while sipping daintily from fine china and out of the earshot of husbands and fathers? Many claimed that tea parties were frivolous, a waste of time. Women retaliated by charging that men spent too much time in taverns, a place forbidden to the so-called fairer sex. "You charge us with drinking at the Tea-Table," one female defender wrote in a letter to a Boston paper, "and cannot we charge you with drinking more unnaturally at a Tavern?"

Given women's consumption of myriad British goods, with tea figuring chief among them, the patriots understood that the participation of their female counterparts was vital to any boycott's success. In 1770, three hundred women in Boston gave up tea (except if needed for medicinal uses) until Parliament repealed the Townshend Acts. Their protest proved ultimately effective despite the sneering of Loyalists who charged that "they could be sick just as suited their Convenience and Inclination" in order to warrant sipping some Bohea.

After Parliament repealed the Townshend duties on goods except tea, most American women resumed their tea-drinking ways, though they usually opted for the smuggled variety that bypassed the tariff. In the wake of the Boston Tea Party, however, women saw the renewed boycotts as a chance to stand alongside men and assert their patriotism. Nowhere was that truer than in two North Carolina towns, Edenton and Wilmington, where, in the fall and winter of 1774, the phrase *tea party* took on a whole new meaning.

Incorporated in 1722, Edenton lies on the northeastern shore of Albemarle Sound, in North Carolina's Inner Banks; at the time of the American Revolution, the town served as the colony's capital. Named after Charles Eden, one of the early governors, it was a wealthy little village of about five hundred, a market town graced with a shipping port convenient for rich planters. Even today, more than two centuries later, Edenton remains a tourist attraction; in 2011 *Forbes* magazine named the quaint hamlet one of America's prettiest towns.

THE EDENTON AND WILMINGTON TEA PARTIES

Most of Edenton's beauty derives from its colonial history, an era when its green lawns spread down to water's edge and the gardens of its Georgian houses, as one early historian recorded, "enclosed bowers of Jessamine and clematis, with thickets of rose and japonicas." In the center of town was a brick courthouse surrounded by a village green. It was a typical, sleepy colonial capital containing, according to an early resident, "a greater number of men eminent for ability, virtue, and learning, than in any other part of America."

The same writer noted that the women of Edenton "were models of virtue, refinement and high-born courage," and when writing those words he may have had Penelope Barker in mind. This American heroine was born in Edenton in 1728 to Samuel Padgett, a prominent doctor, and his wife, Elizabeth, the daughter of a wealthy planter. While still in her early teens, Penelope lost her father and sister, who died within a year of each other. By age sixteen, she had married a planter named John Hodgson and gave birth to two sons in quick succession; Hodgson died when his wife was only nineteen, leaving her to care not only for their two children but also for three children from his previous marriage. Four years later, Penelope wed again, this time to an extremely wealthy planter named James Craven; upon his death, in 1755, she became the wealthiest woman in North Carolina. (She was also reportedly one of the most beautiful.) Two years later she married Thomas Barker, a prominent attorney and member of the North Carolina assembly. Of their three children, none survived even a year. In all, Penelope Barker bore five children of her own and raised four of her husbands' children from other marriages; by 1761, seven of these children were dead. When her son Thomas Hodgson died in 1772, at the age of twenty-five, she was left with only a single living child, a daughter named Betsy Barker.

In other words, Penelope Barker's life was filled with trial, adversity, and death, most of it while she was still a young woman. Such stories were hardly unusual in the colonial era, with its high rates of infant mortality and short life expectancies. In the southern regions, if a person survived to adulthood, he or she might be plagued by climate-borne diseases and could expect to live perhaps forty-eight years (compared to sixty-two for New Englanders). But Barker was obviously made of strong steel tempered in the brutally hot fire of her experience.

Beginning in the early 1760s, Barker's husband became an agent for the North Carolina government and spent a good deal of time in London. At the outbreak of the Revolutionary War, Thomas was trapped there and unable to return home until 1778, and so his wife spent a good deal of time running the family's plantations alone.

Like any prominent North Carolina matron, Barker was responsible for her household's social life, which revolved around

IN THIS BRITISH LAMPOON OF THE EDENTON TEA PARTY, PENELOPE BARKER IS
DRAWN AS A GROTESQUE KING GEORGE WHILE A DOG URINATES AT HER FEET.

quilting bees, cotillion parties, and the afternoon teas she held in her home on Broad Street, which were attended by a large group of women who constituted Edenton's high society. Tea parties were reassuring ceremonies organized according to an exact ritual. After guests had been seated, the boiling water was brought in a large tea caddy to the table. Each guest placed a certain number of tea leaves in her cup, depending on her own preference for strong or weak tea, and then the water was poured over the tea. At that point, the guests placed their saucers on top of the cups to keep the brew warm while it steeped, after which it was ready for drinking.

In the fall of 1774, these popular ceremonies came to an abrupt halt. On September 10, the North Carolina assembly instituted a boycott of all British products, including tea, and, in early October, North Carolina delivered more than 2,000 bushels of corn, 22 barrels of flour, and 17 barrels of pork to a suffering Boston population whose harbor was shut down by the Intolerable Acts. In the middle of that same month, Barker went to her friend Elizabeth King and asked her to invite fifty-one members of Edenton's Ladies Patriotic Guild for a special meeting to be held in King's larger home. On October 25, seven days after the burning of the *Peggy Stewart*, Barker led a meeting in which all fifty-one women decided to affix their names to a document that read, in part:

THE EDENTON AND WILMINGTON TEA PARTIES

We the ladies of Edenton do hereby solemnly en-
gage not to conform to ye pernicious Custom of
Drinking Tea or that we, the aforesaid Ladies, will not
promote ye wear of any manufacture from England,
until such time that all Acts which tend to enslave
this our Native Country shall be repealed.

It was an incredibly bold statement. The women of Edenton were publicly telling the king of England they would not
buy his products as long as he kept their country—*their* country,
not his—in bondage. It was the first such public, organized
women's protest in American history. After the meeting, Barker
supposedly said: "Maybe it has only been men who have
protested the king up to now. That only means we women have
taken too long to let our voices be heard. We are signing our
names to a document, not hiding ourselves behind costumes like
the men in Boston did at their tea party. The British will know
who we are."

To make sure, Barker herself sent the statement to the
Morning Chronicle and London Advertiser, where it appeared on
January 16, 1775, along with a note she had written:

The provincial deputies of North Carolina, having resolved not to drink any more tea, nor wear any British
cloth &c., many ladies of this province have deter-

mined to give a memorable proof of their patriotism, and have, accordingly, entered into the following honourable and spirited association. I send it to you to show our fair countrywomen how zealously and faithfully American ladies follow the laudable example of their husbands and what opposition your matchless ministers may expect to receive from a people thus firmly united against them.

The news caused a tremendous stir in England, in part because so many of the Edenton women—including Barker herself—had husbands or relations working in Britain. Most Englishmen found it absurd that Barker and her cosigners had the temerity to get themselves mixed up in serious political business. One such skeptic was Arthur Iredell, who wrote to his brother James, a prominent North Carolina attorney who later became one of the first associates of the U.S. Supreme Court: "I see by the Newspaper that the Edenton Ladies have signalized themselves by their Protest against Tea-drinking. Is there a Female Congress in Edenton too? I hope not for we Englishmen are afraid of Male Congress, but . . . the Ladies . . . have ever, since the Amazonian Era, been esteemed the most Formidable Enemies; . . . the only Security on our Side to prevent the impending ruin, that I can perceive, is the probability that there are few places in America which possess so much Female Artillery as Edenton."

THE EDENTON AND WILMINGTON TEA PARTIES

In March 1775, cartoonist Philip Dawe published in a London newspaper a mocking woodcut entitled "A Society of Patriotic Ladies at Edenton in North Carolina," in which he drew Penelope Barker as a grotesque female King George III. Underneath the table at which she sat, a dog urinated at her feet while a baby played nearby. It summed up the English view of American colonists—uncouth and uppity.

With her husband away for three years after the outbreak of war, Barker continued to show a great deal of initiative and courage. One story that's still told in North Carolina—but that may be apocryphal—recounts a visit to her plantation made by British troops, who attempted to lead away her prized horse. She came running out with a saber and proceeded to slash the reins. A gallant British officer was impressed by her bravery, and Barker was allowed to keep the steed. Outliving her husband by seven years, Penelope Barker died in 1796, at the age of sixty-eight. She hasn't been much commemorated in American history, except by a merchant ship named after her that had the misfortune of being sunk by a U-boat in 1944 while on a convoy run to Murmansk. And, although Elizabeth King's house—the site of the Edenton women's "tea party"—was torn down in the nineteenth century, a bronze teapot marks the site where it once stood.

Not every city in colonial North Carolina was as civilized as Edenton. The well-born Scottish traveler Janet Schaw, in her wonderfully titled *Journal of a Lady of Quality*, described her ride through the woods of the Cape Fear region of North Carolina in language straight out of a Grimm's fairy tale:

> But by and by it begins to grow dark, and as the idea of being benighted in the wilds of America was not a pleasing circumstance to an European female, I begged the servant to drive faster, but was told it would make little difference, as we must be many hours dark, before we could get clear of the woods, nor were our fears decreased by the stories Mr Eagle told us of the wolves and bears that inhabited that part of the country.

> Terrified at last almost to Agony, we begged to be carried to some house to wait for day-light. . . . We had not gone far in this frightful state, when we found the carriage stopt by trees fallen across the road, and were forced to dismount and proceed thro this dreary scene on foot. All I had ever heard of lions, bears, tigers and wolves now rushed on my memory, and I secretly wished I had been made a feast to the fishes rather than to those monsters of the woods.

Wilmington, North Carolina, was established on the Cape Fear River, some twenty-eight miles upstream from the Atlantic, in a poorly settled portion of the colony. Before being incorporated in 1739—the town was named after the Earl of Wilmington, a patron of Gabriel Johnson, then royal governor of North Carolina—it was variously called New Liverpool, New Town, and Newton. This unclear identity seems fitting, since Wilmington was a magnet for the transplanted and the dispossessed. It was founded by second and third sons of New Englanders who, unable to inherit family land given to first-born sons, had ventured south in the hope of starting farms. Many settlers were Huguenots seeking religious freedom. The community also included thousands of Highland Scots who had left the poor prospects of their native country to settle along the river; Janet Schaw was visiting relatives who had done just that.

A historian once wrote of Wilmington that it "evolved into a backwater town," which gives you some idea of its humble beginnings. One visitor described it as a "poor, Hungry, unprovided Place, consisting of not above 10 or 12 scattering mean houses." Surrounded by swamps and bogs, it was badly situated and far from the ocean. Settlers hoped it might serve as a commerce center for those in the backwoods counties of North Carolina, since the Cape Fear was used as a riverine highway by traders and farmers who navigated in shallow draft boats. But for oceangoing vessels, the river presented daunting shoals and other maneuvering challenges. Further complicating matters, sailors avoided docking in Wilmington because disease was endemic there. Although the town would be revived in the mid-1800s, when the river was dredged and widened and steam engines replaced sails, in prerevolutionary days it was an indeed "unprovided Place."

One thing Wilmington shared with its finer cousin Edenton was a determination not to be cowed by the British. When the Stamp Act was announced in 1765, a mob of several hundred gathered to protest. According to the *South-Carolina Gazette*, a Charleston newspaper covering events in the Carolinas, these patriots "exhibited the effigy of a certain honorable gentleman; and after letting it hang by the neck for some time, near the courthouse they made a large bonfire with a number of tar barrels, etc., and committed it to the flames."

The effigy in question was that of a Scot who expressed his support of the legislation, which was not surprising, given that the Highlanders tended to be Loyalists. As the fire burned, the mob gathered the town's wealthy inhabitants to watch, forcing them to drink a toast to "Liberty, Property and No Stamp Duty." At the end of the month, another mob created an effigy of William Houston, the king's stamp collector, took it in procession to the church graveyard, buried it, dug it up, and dragged it to the town square, where they propped it in an armchair in front of a large bonfire and pretended to toast heartily to its health. Needless to say, when shortly thereafter the real Mr. Houston came to town, he immediately resigned his commission.

THE EDENTON AND WILMINGTON TEA PARTIES

In early 1766, hundreds of men, this time bearing firearms—something Boston patriots would refrain from doing until the battles of Lexington and Concord, some nine years later—boarded two British ships carrying the hated duty stamps and confiscated them. In July 1770, protesting the Townshend Act, the General Committee of the Sons of Liberty met in Wilmington and vowed "to keep strictly to a Non-Importation agreement." So, despite its backwoods, or "rustick" (as Schaw described it in her book), nature, in the 1760s and early 1770s Wilmington was at the forefront of the colonies—and even ahead of some—when it came to protesting British tariffs. And when, in September 1774, the North Carolina assembly instituted a boycott on all British imports, the local chapter of the Sons of Liberty fully supported it.

The next year saw the acerbic Schaw navigating a dark tangle of forests to arrive in Wilmington, and her comments concerning the men of North Carolina are rather unflattering: "They are tall and lean, with short waists and long limbs, sallow complexions and languid eyes, when not inflamed by spirits." She hastened to point out, however, that this description applies only to "the peasantry." She had yet to meet the better sort of man and still had hopes, on arriving at Wilmington, "to find an American Gentleman a very different creature from an American clown." But in this, too, she was to be disappointed. The gentlemen she encountered were mainly radical patriots whose "natural ferocity is now inflamed by the fury of an ignorant zeal.... I cannot look at them without connecting the idea of tar and feather."

Schaw formed an entirely different impression of Wilmington's women, however. On one occasion she accepted an invitation to a ball, only to discover that no carriage would be available to transport her; instead, she would have to walk through "the unpaved streets in embroidered shoes by the light of a lanthorn [lantern] carried by a black wench half naked." It was an inauspicious beginning to the night's entertainments, but, upon arriving at her destination, Schaw was impressed by the female company. "The Ladies were amiable and agreeable," she wrote, "and would make a figure in any part of the world."

Having befriended some of these impressive ladies, Schaw was surprised to walk out upon the muddy streets of Wilmington one day in late winter 1775 and see a long line of women approaching the town square. They were all holding small boxes, and, as Schaw approached, she realized the boxes contained tea. The women gathered in a circle on the village green, where they dumped the contents into a pile—and then set fire to it.

Were it not for Janet Schaw passing by that day, we might never have known about the quiet yet forceful Wilmington Tea Party. According to her, the event didn't amount to much:

> The Ladies have burnt their tea in solemn procession, but had delayed however til the sacrifice was

not very considerable, as I do not think any one offered above a quarter of a pound. . . .

All the Merchants of any note are [Scottish] and Irish,
and many of them very genteel people. They all disapprove of the present proceedings. Many of them
intend quitting the country as fast as their affairs will
permit them, but are yet uncertain what steps to take.

In fact, the small fire amounted to a great deal. Although
Penelope Barker and the women of Edenton had risked much by
publicly proclaiming their boycott of tea, the women of Wilmington had gone further still—they had *burned* the stuff, destroying it
in a gesture at once more violent and symbolic. In that sense, they
resembled their gentlemen counterparts, whom Schaw so despised
for being "inflamed by the fury of an ignorant zeal." Perhaps that
is why, disappointed with her new "lady friends," Schaw impugns
their motives by claiming they burned only the smallest possible
amount of tea. Shortly thereafter she moved on, and there ends our
glimpse of the patriotic women of Wilmington. It seems obvious,
in retrospect, that the Scottish traveler had missed something crit-
ical in her observations: If women in Wilmington, of all places, were
lining up to burn their tea in public, then the message of the patriots had successfully spread to the most remote and inhospitable
corners of the American colonies.

CHAPTER TEN

The Greenwich
Tea Party

December 1774

"The people seem indeed
to be full of patriotic fire."

From the journal of Philip Vickers Fithian

Ask anyone to cite the most pivotal colonies in the American Revolution, and the same three names always come up: Massachusetts (site of the battles of Lexington and Concord), Pennsylvania (birthplace of the Declaration of Independence), and Virginia (home to both George Washington and Thomas Jefferson).

New Jersey, as usual, gets no respect. Yet it was there that an important (albeit disreputable) form of colonial civil disobedience took place during the years before the revolution: smuggling.

The forests of South Jersey—incredibly dense and thick, with huge cedars and thousands of acres of pine trees—were a hotbed of surreptitious importation, offering natural hideouts for those seeking to subvert British law. Inhabitants of these areas were mythically tough and hulking men who appeared and disappeared like a miasma of swamp gas; law-abiding neighbors often described them as "Swamp Men" or "Swamp Angels."

But the denizens of these "smuggler's woods," as the South Jersey coastal woodlands came to be known, were no angels.

They stole valuable lumber from their neighbors' land, illegally manufactured pine tar and turpentine in rough and lonely backwoods factories, robbed travelers on the region's rough roads, and joined privateers' crews based inland along the rivers that led to the ocean from the deep woods—the Mullica and the Cohansey were two of the main smuggler conduits. By the mid-1700s, the area had attracted many settlers from New England, who brought with them their shrewd trading and sophisticated knowledge of smuggling. Valuable contraband—sugar, china, tea, fabric—found its way to Little Egg Harbor, Tom's River, Cape May, and down rivers to remote settlements deep in the interior, where it was loaded onto wagons and mules and transported overland to Philadelphia, Burlington, and other urban centers.

British laws prohibiting smuggling had always existed, although, until the end of the French and Indian War, they were generally unenforced. Everyone smuggled, from the lowest Swamp Angel to men of substance, including Boston's John Hancock and Philadelphia merchant James Logan, a Quaker. After the French and Indian War, British Parliament, in its disastrous attempt to tax the colonies, not only placed a higher duty on much-desired items like sugar and tea—effectively encouraging more smuggling—it also hired new customs collectors to try to enforce the laws already on the books.

The results—especially in southern New Jersey—weren't

pretty. The first step was to fire the old customs inspectors, who, it was widely known, made most of their money from bribery, looking the other way as smuggled goods passed by. They were replaced by Scotsmen, who supposedly could squeeze a shilling far enough to survive on their paltry official salaries. Immune to bribes, the new inspectors found themselves under constant assault. One customs informant was tarred, feathered, pilloried, and ducked in the ocean, after which he was "let go in peace, to sin no more." The inspector for Cape May, who'd had the temerity to confiscate smuggled goods, was captured by a mob, beaten, and tarred and feathered. Then, according to another customs collector who viewed the scene, "the mob gathered as they drove him with sticks from Street to Street. They had a rope round his body, and when he could not walk or run, they drag'd him." The observer concluded: "I am much at a loss what steps to take in this matter. Many people here say they are sorry for what has happened, tho' I believe most in their hearts approve of it."

A favorite port for "connoisseurs of contraband," as historian Arthur D. Pierce calls them, was Greenwich, New Jersey, about forty-five miles south of Philadelphia. It was—and, to some extent, still is—a remote and scenic spot on the banks of the Cohansey River, about five miles inland from Delaware Bay. Planned in 1676 by John Fenwick, a Quaker merchant, around "Ye Greate Street"—a thoroughfare a mile long and a hundred feet wide—the town was completed by land speculators, including William Penn, after Fenwick's death. It was known as Cohansey until the 1690s, when a group of settlers arrived from New England and renamed it Greenwich, after the Connecticut town. By the early 1700s, it had become one of New Jersey's three official ports of entry, along with Perth Amboy and Burlington. A bustling ship-building, farming, and merchant center, Greenwich featured, according to one early-twentieth-century writer, "an active, energetic and God-fearing people" who attended Presbyterian or Quaker churches but kept the small town's seven taverns in business as well.

However they may have feared God, the people of Greenwich smuggled to their hearts' content. As early as 1714, a petition signed by thirty-four local men protested against paying a tax that would support Crown officials:

> Wee whose Names are under Written do Utterly
>   Denie to pay
> or Suffer to be taken by Distress or any other ways
>   any money
> Goods or any other thing by Francis Pagit our so
>   called Constable
> Because wee Doubt of his Being a Lawful Constable
>   & more especially
> Because wee have been Illegally Assessed.

THE GREENWICH TEA PARTY

This was no idle protest. The petition signers were indicted for refusing to pay the "so called Constable," although records are unclear whether they were ever brought to trial. Nevertheless, they made the job of constable so unattractive that, when the court named Jonathan Holmes as sheriff, he refused to take the job and was thrown in jail for noncompliance.

Today in Greenwich there still exists the Pyrate's House, which was built in 1734 and probably did indeed house pirates, who were numerous at the time. At just a half hour's sail up the Cohansey, Greenwich would have been the perfect place for the brigands to unload their ill-gotten gains. Tea was among the most commonly smuggled goods; after being received in Greenwich, it was shipped overland to Philadelphia and Burlington. Even after the passage of the Intolerable Acts in the spring of 1774—after which radicals up and down the East Coast were calling for a boycott of *all* tea—there was still an underground market for Bohea. Life in Greenwich was business as usual.

And so it remained until October 1774, when a young would-be clergyman named Philip Vickers Fithian rode into town. Fithian was returning home from Virginia, where he'd been employed as a tutor for the children of a wealthy planter. Born to grain farmers, young Philip experienced a religious conversion, attended Princeton, was ordained a minister, rode the circuit in the wilds of New Jersey and Pennsylvania, and, ultimately, became a chaplain to George Washington's army, dying a premature death from disease in 1776. He was an inveterate, sharp-eyed diarist, and his journals capture rich details of his colonial-era life, from the agonies of a toothache to the eyes of a pretty country girl watching him as he undressed before bed in a one-room backwoods cabin.

On his way home to Greenwich that autumn, Fithian passed through Annapolis, where he witnessed the dramatic climax of its tea party—the fiery burning of the brig *Peggy Stewart*. He recorded in his journal that "the people seem indeed to be full of patriotic fire" and then went on his way. Upon arriving in Greenwich, he waxed eloquent to his friends about the events he'd seen in Annapolis. It seemed hard to imagine anything similar happening in their quiet country village.

But then, late on the night of December 12, a British brig docked at Greenwich wharf. The *Greyhound* came bearing a large shipment of East India Company tea. After making the Atlantic crossing, Captain Allen had met a Delaware River pilot at Lewes, Delaware, who warned him that bringing his cargo of tea into Philadelphia would be a suicidal act, given the temper of the city and the incidents involving Captain Ayres almost a year before. Allen decided to take his ship down the Cohansey River instead and land it in Greenwich, where he could meet with a Tory named Dan Bowen, a former sea captain he'd known years earlier. It was agreed that Bowen would, for a price, hide the tea in his home near the wharf until the merchandise was ready to be smuggled overland to Philadelphia. Although Bowen was not at home on the fateful night (possibly by prearrangement), the tea was delivered and unloaded into his cellar.

This delicate undercover operation was supposed to remain a secret; within a few days, however, the entire town knew about the hidden tea. On December 18, Fithian wrote in his journal:

> Early last week a Quantity of Tea said to be shipped at Rotterdam was brought & privately stored at Dan Bowen's in Greenwich—a pro Tempore Committee was chosen to secure it til the County Committee be duly elected.

One of the great ironic notes in the entire Greenwich narrative is that this town, which owed so much of its existence to smuggling, was now trying to stop legal tea from being smuggled.

The young men of the village were swept up in a patriotic frenzy and, on Thursday, December 22, called a mass meeting in nearby Bridgeton. After deliberations, members decided that "being ignorant of the principles on which the tea was imported, from whence it came, or the importers' names . . . [it was] best to have it privately stored."

The decision was an extremely cautious and proper one, and, not surprisingly, the young men of Greenwich disagreed entirely. So, that evening, twenty-three of them made their way, singly and in small groups, to the home of Philip Vickers Fithian. When the men left, as Arthur Pierce describes it, "they were disguised, or at least dressed, as Indians." Carrying torches, the men then proceeded directly to Market Square, where they planned to liberate the tea. (It's uncertain whether Bowen had returned home during all the commotion; it appears he'd made himself scarce.) Facing no obstacles at Bowen's house, the Indians entered the cellar and dragged out the chests, pulling them across Ye Greate Street to the village green. Within minutes, the tea was being roasted. Dry from long storage, it burned quickly, and the smell wafted over the town and to the countryside beyond. If the scent didn't wake the inhabitants of Greenwich, the noise certainly did, for the young men were cavorting around the fire, whooping and hollering, just as they imagined real Indians might.

As at other tea parties, there was one participant who couldn't resist attempting to save a little tea for himself. His name was Henry Stacks, the son of a local surveyor, and he began quietly stuffing his pockets. When no one seemed to notice, he tied his pants at the ankles and poured tea down his trousers. By this time, he was carrying so much tea that his clothes ballooned; his fellow "Indians" noticed and forced him to dump it in the fire. Unlike tea thief Captain O'Connor in Boston—who was beaten as he tried to run away—Stacks was merely scolded. Known the rest of his life as "Tea-Stacks," he actually became a prosperous landowner in nearby Dutch Neck.

The next day, Fithian wrote in his journal:

> Last night the tea was, by a number of persons in disguise, taken out of the house & consumed with fire. Violent and different are the words about this uncommon Manoeuvre, among the Inhabitants. Some rave, some curse & condemn, some try to reason, many are glad the Tea is destroyed, but almost all disapprove the manner of destruction.

Since most historians accept that Philip Vickers Fithian was one of the "Indians" involved in the "violent" act, his journal entry shouldn't be taken at face value—it was probably a way to cover himself should his identity come to light. The same could be said for the committee, which met the same day that Fithian was making his journal entry, and resolved that "we entirely disapprove of the destroying of the tea it being entirely contrary to our resolves . . . we will not conceal nor protect from justice any of the perpetrators of the above act."

Of course, at least three members of the abovementioned committee—Joel Fithian (Philip's cousin), Silas Newcomb, and Thomas Ewing—were among the tea burners. They were wise to be discreet about their identities, for the East India Company would later bring suit against them through its Philadelphia agents, John Duffield and Stacy Hepburn, requesting £1,200 in damages. Moreover, the company targeted specific group members, including Newcomb, his brother Ephraim, and Richard Howell. This outcome was exactly the one dreaded by those who had dumped the tea in Boston Harbor; indeed, a man could be ruined by a suit brought on by the EIC. The tea burners lawyered up accordingly. Funds were raised to help with their legal defense, and they secured some fairly distinguished attorneys—Joseph Bloomfield, who later became governor of New Jersey, and Jonathan D. Sergeant, of Philadelphia, who served in the Continental Congress.

It would have made for a fascinating court case, with eloquent and distinguished lawyers on both sides arguing the facts. The arguments for and against the East India Company had never been tried in a court of law. The benefits to history of such a trial transcript would have been invaluable.

Of course, the lawyers for the tea burners were interested not in history but in their clients, and they continued to delay the trial until after the battles of Lexington and Concord had taken place. By that point, the American Revolution was under way, and the British had lost any judicial influence over New Jersey.

Nevertheless, the Loyalist New Jersey governor, William Franklin, through a local judge, attempted to bring criminal charges against the tea burners by convening a grand jury to indict them. The judge, as one of the tea burners present wrote, "gave a very Large Charge to the Grand Jury Concerning the times & the burning of the tea," but the grand jury, sensing which way the winds were blowing, refused to return an indictment. The judge stubbornly convened yet another jury, but it had been deliberately packed with patriots by the foreman, the brother of one of the tea burners. No indictment was forthcoming.

The tea burners of Greenwich would prove to be a remarkably accomplished group. Their ranks included a future governor (Richard Howell) and a future member of the U.S. House of Representatives (Ebenezer Elmer). Also in their ranks were three future state legislators and four future doctors. Most of these men enlisted in the Continental Army, and four would die in the service of their country.

New Jersey gave us the last of the colonial-era tea parties. It seems fitting that the tea demonstrations ended as they began, with "Indians" destroying East India Company tea in a wild frenzy. By the nineteenth century, Greenwich had lost its importance as a market town and smuggler's haven as new roads were built elsewhere, leaving the village passed by on its marshy peninsula—one reason why so much of the town and its surrounding farmlands have been preserved as though the calendar still read 1774.

Epilogue

"If you read our founding fathers, people like Franklin and Jefferson, what we're doing in this country now is making them roll over in their graves."

—CNN reporter Rick Santelli, February 19, 2009

U nlike the battles of Lexington and Concord, or Washington's crossing of the Delaware, or the signing of the Declaration of Independence, America's early tea parties produced no revolutionary heroes, monuments, odes, or fulsome congressional declarations of thanks. Even the phrase *tea party* didn't come in to use until the 1830s; before then, the events of the evening of December 16, 1773, that took place on Griffin's Wharf in Boston were generally known as "the action against the tea" or "the destruction of the tea." Those who participated in the raid were called "tea destroyers."

There were good reasons for the silence. The men who tossed 92,000 pounds of tea into Boston Harbor knew they were at great risk of being arrested. In an era when a simple burglary was a hanging offense, one did not want to be caught destroying £9,659 worth of prime East India Company goods. Even the rich and powerful John Hancock, one of the planners of the Boston Tea Party, wrote in its aftermath: "Indeed, I am not acquainted with [the incident] myself so as to give a detail."

TEN TEA PARTIES

After the war had been waged and the colonies emerged victorious, it's conceivable the tea destroyers would have let down their guard (and, heck, maybe even boasted a little). But most still feared recrimination, specifically lawsuits from the East India Company, a large and historically vengeful entity. After all, the East India Company had already filed suit against the Greenwich patriots, and the men of New Jersey had destroyed a lot less tea than what the Mohawks dumped into Boston Harbor.

Local officials also sought to keep the mayhem wrought by the tea parties under wraps. After all, what sort of government celebrates mob violence? After the American Revolution, the last thing the founding fathers wanted were angry gangs taking issue with taxation. Leaders like John Adams, Alexander Hamilton, George Washington, and Thomas Jefferson knew all too well that a single incident—an unpopular law, the arrival of an arrogant tax collector—could spark a riot that brought down a venerable institution, never mind a nascent democracy. (A prime example of the type of unrest the founders dreaded was the Whiskey Rebellion of the early 1790s, when an angry group of five hundred armed Pennsylvanians attacked the home of a government official trying to collect an excise tax on whiskey.) Although the Boston Tea Party and those that followed resulted in no loss of life, the protests were nevertheless violent. People were threatened, their property was destroyed, and their families were terrified. In the new United States, there was no room for mobs on the street or neighbors attacking neighbors.

It wasn't until the 1820s and '30s that the cloak of silence began to unravel as Americans tried to shape the narrative of their rebellion. Beginning around 1835, in books and newspaper articles describing the events, the destruction of the tea came to be dubbed "the Tea Party," although the word *party* was meant in the sense of a faction or group, rather than a celebration. This was a time of labor unrest in America. Workers were marching and striking for a ten-hour work day, and their leaders started evoking the Boston Tea Party as a salutary example of what could be accomplished through civil disobedience. At the same time, much of the violence that had taken place before and during the Boston Tea Party was softened or ignored. This process, called "taming the event" by historian Alfred F. Young, allows controversial incidents to be written into histories for schoolchildren. In many ways, this taming is still with us to this day, since so few Americans seem aware of the true nature of the original tea party protests.

By the 1830s, the few surviving tea partiers were being feted in public. The apprentice cobbler George Robert Twelves Hughes, who lived to be nearly a hundred years old, was the subject of two biographies. In a portrait painted by Boston artist Joseph Cole, Hughes's likeness presents an intrepid gentleman with a wise and aged face, certainly not a man capable of mob violence. There was even the obligatory tea party imposter—

David Kinnison (or Kennison), who died in Chicago in 1852, at the supposed age of 115, after convincing the people of that good city that he had actively participated in the Boston Tea Party, despite being only eight years old in 1773.

As the tea parties receded into the past, they were increasingly adopted as a symbol for political action. For the centennial of the Boston Tea Party, in 1873, suffragettes staged raucous women's rights rallies in that city, New York, and Philadelphia—all sites of eighteenth-century tea parties. In Boston, the Young Women's Christian Association featured women dressed in "ye old colonial costumes," serving tea to "young Mohawks in the dress of their native tribe" and passing out miniature souvenir tea chests. By 1919, when a crowd of fifty thousand chanting anti-Prohibitionists held a rally on Boston Common (which was advertised by local pubs and labor unions alike), the Boston Tea Party had fully assumed its dual identity as circus event and protest template.

Since then, the tea party has been co-opted by countless groups with conflicting viewpoints. "Our nation in a sense came into being through a massive act of civil disobedience, for the Boston Tea Party was nothing but a massive act of civil disobedience," wrote Martin Luther King in his 1963 "Letter from a Birmingham Jail." Yet, that same event had been recalled in the 1920s by the imperial wizard of the Ku Klux Klan, who claimed that the "Ku Klux spirit" was present at the Boston Tea Party

EPILOGUE

and that it had animated the tea destroyers. Indian leader Mahatma Gandhi compared his actions to those of the Boston Tea Party as well, as did Chinese revolutionary Sun Yat-sen. On the other side of the coin, white conservatives in Rhodesia (present-day Zambia) protested the actions of postwar black revolutionaries there, saying, in the words of one such conservative, "there must never again be another 'Boston tea party' with its deplorable sequel."

Tea party mania may have reached its zenith during the bicentennial celebration of the Boston Tea Party, in 1973. On Saturday, December 16, forty thousand people marched through rain and snow to the Boston waterfront Reenactors wearing tricornes and knee breeches dumped tea into the harbor from a replica of the East India Company ship *Beaver*, with the whole hoopla sponsored by the tea company Salada. Afterward, the *Beaver* was boarded by another group that unfurled a sign reading: DUMP NIXON, NOT TEA. That same group, some wearing Nixon masks, tarred and feathered an effigy of Nixon and hung him from the ship's yardarm. Next to board the ship were members of the Disabled Veterans of America, dressed as Indians; this group was immediately followed by members of Boston's Indian Council, who were protesting the Native American disguises. Back on shore, members of the National Organization for Women marched in support of the Equal Rights Amendment, while other demonstrators carried banners and placards supporting grape strikers, Greek students, and the Gay American Revolution. Still more signs denounced the coup in Chile, the war in Vietnam, and alleged profiteering of oil companies. The next day, an editorial in the *Washington Post* sniffed that the event had been "artificially contrived and concocted . . . [and was] distinguished by commercial and ideological hucksterism." In other words, it was a classic American tea party.

Today, the Tea Party is a full-fledged political movement, although it consists of several groups, large and small, not all of whom agree with one another. Some are Republicans, some are libertarians, and some are conservative independents fed up with both major parties. Tea Party members almost universally share a reverence for the founding fathers and (according to their critics) a simplified view of said founders' motivation. It can be tempting, for example, to understate how carefully John Hancock and Samuel Adams managed and manipulated working-class mobs to create incidents—including the Boston Tea Party—that would ultimately serve their ends.

The modern Tea Party movement was born on February 19, 2009, with CNN reporter Rick Santelli's famous rant on the floor of the Chicago Board of Trade. Santelli criticized then newly elected president Barack Obama for the Homeowner's Affordability and Stability Plan, which helped millions of homeowners avoid foreclosure. He castigated the homeowners, calling them "losers," and asked viewers if they really wanted to pay for someone else's "extra bathroom." He ended by threatening to launch a Chicago Tea Party as a means of protest.

It was a tough time for the American economy, much as the years leading up to the Revolutionary War had been harsh on the colonists. Then, as now, many citizens were concerned with onerous taxes, oppressive social legislation, and the usurpation of basic rights. But does the current Tea Party truly reflect the values of the tea parties of the early 1770s? To a great extent, this question cannot be answered—the gulf in culture, politics, and people's mind-sets between 1773 and today is simply too vast. Yet similarities do exist; for example, colonial tea partiers protested unfair taxes, as many Tea Partiers do today, and both groups have as their foundation the belief that government is no longer responsive to the will of the people.

Certainly, tea partiers old and new share a sense of moral outrage. In 1773, the East India Company and the British government thought they could buy off the American people by lowering the price of tea by a few shillings and then levying a tax when consumers weren't looking. When Goldman Sachs was bailed out, many saw it as just another example of a special-interest group—much like the East India Company—receiving favorable treatment at the expense of ordinary people powerless to do anything about it.

Most Tea Party constituents have a good grasp of the events that occurred during the Boston Tea Party, but they would do well to understand the details of the other patriotic protests described in this book. All are remarkable, because each town staged its protest in its own unique way. Patriots burned tea in Greenwich and Wilmington and Annapolis; made it disappear (and reappear) in York; dumped it overboard in New York and Charleston; and rejected it in Philadelphia and Edenton. And all manner of people participated in the protests. The working-class laborers of Manhattan, the distinguished ladies of Edenton, the mysterious Swamp Men of Greenwich—all were united behind a common cause. For the first time in the nation's history, Americans banded together *as Americans*.

Later, after the protests and the bloodshed and the Revolutionary War, when people returned once again to drinking tea, it was on their own terms. And I suspect that those steaming cups of Bohea must have tasted pretty good.

Appendix

Even More
Tea Parties

"The carrying of India Tea into the Hall is found to be a Source of uneasiness and grief to many of the students . . ."

—*Faculty records of Harvard College, March 1, 1775*

In the months following the Boston Tea Party, colonial newspapers were filled with accounts of other towns—especially, but not exclusively, those in New England—boycotting, drowning, or burning tea. These events became so commonplace that most merited only a quick mention in the local papers, as in this sentence from the Boston Gazette of January 24, 1774: "Last Thursday, a large Quantity of Bohea Tea given up by some Gentleman was committed to Flames in King-Street."

There were probably far more tea parties than we'll ever know, but here are a few more of the most interesting ones.

December 12, 1773
Lexington, Massachusetts

On the same day as the Boston Tea Party, the *Massachusetts Spy* wrote that the citizens of Lexington "had unanimously resolved against the use of Bohea tea of all sorts, Dutch or English importation" and, to prove their sincerity, gathered all their tea and burned it in public—making this the very first tea party in American history.

TEN TEA PARTIES

December 28, 1773
Charlestown, Massachusetts

An orderly town of small houses with lawns divided by picket fences, Charlestown was the original Puritan settlement on the Boston peninsula, affording sweeping views of the city from its hilly prominences. Charlestown's artisans and middle-class shopkeepers hated the British with a passion. (And the feeling was mutual—after the bloody battle of Bunker Hill in June of 1775, vengeful redcoats put the town to the torch, destroying a large portion.)

But some eighteen months earlier, on December 28, 1773, according to the *Boston Gazette*: "The inhabitants of Charlestown, agreeable to a unanimous Vote of said Town the Tuesday preceding, on Friday last bro't *all* their TEA into the public Market Square, where it was committed to the Flames at high Noon-Day."

December, 1773
Provincetown, Massachusetts

On the night of December 10, 1773, the brig *William*, one of the four original tea ships that the East India Company had sent to Boston, ran aground in the treacherous waters off Cape Cod. Aboard the ship were 300 street lamps destined for the city of Boston as well as 58 chests of tea designated for consignee Richard Clarke. The ship's captain, Joseph Loring, managed to offload all the chests safely. On December 16, the day of the Boston Tea Party, Richard Clarke's son Jonathan left his place of safety with the British on Castle Island, secretly stole away to the Cape Cod location where Loring had hidden the tea, and paid laborers to cart the chests to Provincetown.

From there, the persuasive young Clarke managed to convince the captain of a fishing vessel to carry the tea into Boston Harbor, where it was stored safely in the army fort on Castle Island, thus becoming the only East India tea to land safely in Boston. Upon receiving the news, Sam Adams and the rest of the patriots fumed.

The affair offered a certain consolation, however. While in Provincetown, Jonathan Clarke had sold several chests of the tea to his cousin, a Wellfleet justice of the peace named John Greenough, whose father and half-brother David were prominent Boston patriots. Upon hearing the news, David wrote urgently:

Dear Brother,

The report was brought here today by some credible men from Truro, that very much surprised me as well as all other of your friends, that you were going to bring one or two chests of that cursed tea to Wellfleet itself, which I earnestly beseech you, as your friend and brother, as you value your own interest and the credit of our family, not to concern your self in anyway with the tea. If you have bought any I advise you rather to sink it in the sea than to bring any of it here. For my part I can hardly believe that such a good friend to your country as you always professed to be will shift sides so quickly at the prospect of a little profit.

It was too late. Seven "Indians" showed up at the house in Provincetown where Greenough had hidden one chest of tea; the men seized and burned it. Later, at a town meeting in Wellfleet, the Sons of Liberty demanded and received the other two chests and likewise destroyed them.

Extremely upset, John Greenough wrote to his father in Boston: "Can we imagine a more absolute state of Tyranny and outrageous cruelty than when every private gang of Plunderers and Assassins may wreak their vengeance against any Person or their Property?"

December 31, 1773
Dorchester, Massachusetts
On December 17, 1773—the day after the Boston Tea Party—an elderly laborer named Ebenezer Withington was walking along the salt marshes of a Dorchester beach when he spied a half chest of tea bobbing in the water. Withington knew nothing about either the tea party or the boycott and merely considered himself extraordinarily lucky to have found such a bonanza.

Snatching up the chest, he headed home, although not before encountering a group of Loyalist gentlemen who asked him if he had been "picking up the Ruins," that is, scavenging for any tea that might have floated to shore.

A puzzled Withington asked "if there was any Harm" in what he was doing, to which the gentlemen merely laughed, saying that he had nothing to fear "except from [his] Neighbours." Still perplexed, Withington went home with the tea, drank some, and apparently sold a portion to a few neighbors. The Sons of Liberty heard about his dealings pretty quickly. On December 31, dressed as Narragansett Indians, they raided a home belonging to Withington's two sons. After a search turned up nothing, they continued on to Withington's house, which, according to the *Boston Gazette*, was located "at a place called Sodom." They found the offending weed, seized it, and carried it to Boston. There, in an account provided by prominent Boston merchant John Rowe, the Indians "brought [the tea] into the Commons of Boston & Burnt it this night about eleven o'clock. This is supposed to be part of the Tea that was taken out of the Ships & floated over to Dorchester."

A few days after this nice New Year's Eve blaze, poor Withington was made to face the "Freeholders and other Inhabitants" of Dorchester in a public meeting and recount the story of his finding the tea. Suitably chastened, "old Withingon," as he is often referred to in the accounts, was released without punishment after the citizens decided that his actions had "proceeded from inadvertency."

January, 1774
Princeton, New Jersey

Princeton student Charles Clinton Beatty wrote in a letter to a friend: "Last week to show our patriotism, we gathered all the Steward's winter store of Tea, and having made a fire in the Campus, we then burned near a dozen pounds, tolled the bell, and made many spirited resolves. But this was not all. Poor Mr. (Gov.) Hutchinson's Effigy [Thomas Hutchinson, Governor of Massachusetts] shared the same fate with the Tea, having a Tea canister tied about his neck." Having had a few drinks (and not of tea), Beatty and about forty of his fellow students went into the town "drest in white," pounded on the doors of those known to be tea drinkers, and demanded their tea. Everything they collected was burned.

This escapade may have had the air of a student prank, but it was viewed seriously by Princeton authorities, who denied at least one participant the honor of being Latin salutatorian upon his graduation. Beatty left Princeton in 1775 and joined a Pennsylvania regiment fighting the British but was killed the next year, after a fellow soldier's musket discharged accidentally.

APPENDIX

March 7, 1774
The Second Boston Tea Party

On March 6, 1774, the brig *Fortune* arrived from London carrying twenty-eight and a half chests of Bohea, which was consigned to various Boston merchants including the 120-year-old importing firm of Davison Newman & Co., Ltd. This tea was not shipped directly by the East India Company but rather by other London merchants, and apparently the *Fortune's* captain Benjamin Gorham and the consignees believed that this technicality would keep their cargo from being destroyed by patriots.

No such luck. As the *Boston Gazette* crowed: "The SACHEMS must have a talk upon this matter." They didn't talk long. On March 7, according to a petition for redress that the firm of Davison Newman later sent to King George, "persons, all unknown to the Captain, armed with axes" boarded the *Fortune* "and with force threw the tea in the Water whereby the same was wholly lost and destroyed." The event became known as the Second Boston Tea Party.

November 7, 1774
Yorktown, Virginia

In August 1774, in response to the Boston Tea Party and subsequent Intolerable Acts, Virginia formed a Revolutionary Council that adopted a motion to refuse to purchase any English goods, including tea. In late October, a shipment of tea from

London reached Yorktown aboard the brig *Virginia*. When patriot leaders learned about the cargo, they took quick action. According to the *Virginia Gazette*:

> The inhabitants of York having been informed that the *Virginia*, commanded by Howard Esten, had on Board two Half Chests of Tea, shipped by John Norton, Esq; and Sons, Merchants in London, by Order of Mess. Prentis and Company, Merchants in Williamsburg, assembled at 10 o'clock this Morning, and went on Board the said Ship . . . they immediately hoisted the Tea out of the Hold and threw it into the River, and then returned to the Shore without Damage to the Ship or any other Part of her Cargo.

In May 1775, John Norton, the owner of the *Virginia*, defended his actions in a letter—written from the safety of London—published in the same paper. He stated that he believed the Virginia convention's resolutions "were preparatory only to those intended at the general meeting in August that they were then to receive a sanction from the Congress." He agreed "that the Parliament of Great Britain have not the least shadow of right to tax America; that I never will, directly or indirectly, deviate from these principles . . . which ought to govern every person that has any regard for the liberty of America." One can hear the clacking of yet another merchant's buckled shoes backpedalling in the face of patriot opposition.

March 1, 1775
Cambridge, Massachusetts

Perhaps less a tea party than a college food fight, the event described below was documented in a reprimand noted in Harvard College's faculty records on March 1, 1775:

A Disorder having arisen this morning in the Hall [Harvard Hall] at breakfast between some of the Students, respecting the drinking of India Tea, & some of the Utensils for breakfasting having been broke; & the Parties having been heard—

Resolved 1: We disapprove of the conduct on both sides as imprudent.

Resolved 2: That the regulation of the Hall belongs exclusively to the Government of the College & consequently that no Students have a right to interpose with regard thereunto. . . .

Resolved 3: Since the carrying of India Tea into the Hall is found to be a Source of uneasiness and grief to many of the Students and as the use of it is disagreeable to the People of the Country in general; & as those who carried Tea into the Hall declare that the drinking of it in the Hall is a matter of trifling consequence with them; that they be advised not to carry it in for the future, & and in this way that they, as well as the other

Students in all ways, discover a disposition to promote harmony, mutual affection, and Confidence, so well becoming Members of the same Society . . . whatever convulsions may unhappily distract the State abroad.

BIBLIOGRAPHY

Andrews, Frank D. *The Tea-Burners of Cumberland County.* Cumberland County, N.J.: Vineland Press, 1908.

Block, Lawrence. *Gangsters, Swindlers, Killers and Thieves: The Lives and Crimes of Fifty American Villains.* New York: Oxford University Press, 2004.

Breen, T. H. *The Marketplace of the Revolution: How Consumer Politics Shaped American Independence.* New York: Oxford University Press, 2005.

Burrows, Edwin G., and Mike Wallace. *Gotham: A History of New York City to 1898.* New York: Oxford University Press, 1999.

Carney, Richard. "Edenton Tea Party." http://www.northcarolinahistory.org/commentary/50/entry.

Carp, Benjamin L. *Defiance of the Patriots: The Boston Tea Party & the Making of America.* New Haven: Yale University Press, 2010.

Chidsey, Donald Barr. *The Great Separation: The Story of the Boston Tea Party and the Beginning of the American Revolution.* New York: Crown Publishers, 1965.

Claiborne, Jack, and William Price. *Discovering North Carolina: A Tar Heel Reader.* Chapel Hill: The University of North Carolina Press, 1993.

Colonial Society of Massachusetts. *Publications of the Colonial Society of Massachusetts.* Vol. 8. Boston, Mass., 1902–4.

Copeland, David A. *Debating the Issues in Colonial Newsletters: Primary Documents on Events of the Period.* Westport, Conn.: Greenwood Press, 2000.

Daughters of the American Revolution. *The North Carolina Booklet.* Chapel Hill: The North Carolina Society, 1906.

Dillard, Richard, M.D. *The Historic Tea-Party of Edenton, October 25, 1774: An Incident in North Carolina Connected with British Taxation.* Roanoke, Va.: Roanoke Memorial Society: 1908.

Drake, Francis Samuel. *Tea Leaves: Being a Collection of Letters and Documents Relating to the Shipment of Tea to the American Colonies in the Year 1773.* Boston: A. O. Crane, 1884.

Etting, Frank Marx. *An Historical Account of the Old State House of Pennsylvania.* Boston: James Osgood, 1876.

Fraser, Walter, Jr. *Patriots, Pistols and Petticoats: "Poor Sinful Charles Town" During the American Revolution.* Columbia: University of South Carolina Press, 1976.

Goldbold, Stanly E., and Robert H. Woody. *Christopher Gadsden and the American Revolution.* Knoxville: The University of Tennessee Press, 1982.

Goodheart, Adam. "Tea and Fantasy." *The American Scholar,* October 26, 2005.

Griswold, Wesley S. *The Night the Revolution Began: The Boston Tea Party, 1773.* Brattleboro, Vt.: The Stephen Greene Press, 1972.

Higgins, Pat. "The Tea Party at York, Maine." http://www.imaginemaine

.com/ImagineMaine/Tea_Party.html.

Kammen, Michael. *Colonial New York: A History*. New York: Charles Scribner's Sons, 1975.

Ketchum, Richard M. *Divided Loyalties: How the American Revolution Came to New York*. New York: Henry Holt, 2002.

Leamon, James S. *Revolution Downeast: The War for American Independence in Maine*. Portland: The Maine Historical Society, 1993.

Lepore, Jill. *The Whites of Their Eyes: The Tea Party's Revolution and the Battle Over American History*. Princeton: Princeton University Press, 2010.

McDonough, Daniel J. *Christopher Gadsden and Henry Laurens: The Parallel Lives of Two American Patriots*. Susquehanna, Pa.: Susquehanna University Press, 2000.

Pierce, *Arthur. Smugglers' Woods: Jaunts and Journeys in Colonial and Revolutionary New Jersey*. Piscataway, N.J.: Rutgers University Press, 1964.

Russell, David Lee. *The American Revolution in the Southern Colonies*. New York: McFarland, 2000.

Sprunt, James. *Chronicles of the Cape Fear River, 1660–1916*. Raleigh: Raleigh, Edwards and Durham, 1916.

Taylor, Alan. *American Colonies*. New York: Viking Press, 2001.

Treese, Lorett. *The Storm Gathering: The Penn Family and the American Revolution*. University Park: Penn State University Press, 1992.

Ukers, William H. *All about Tea*. 2 vols. New York: The Tea and Coffee Trade Journal Co., 1935.

Weigley, Russell Frank and Edwin Wolf. *Philadelphia: A 300-Year History*. New York: W. W. Norton, 1982.

Wilber, Marguerite Eyer. *The East India Company and the British Empire in the Far East*. New York: Richard R. Smith, 1945.

Wild, Antony. *The East India Company: Trade and Conquest from 1600*. New York: Lyons Press, 2000.

Young, Alfred F. *The Shoemaker and the Tea Party: Memory and the American Revolution*. Boston: Beacon Press, 2000.

INDEX

INDEX

INDEX

PHOTO CREDITS

All interior illustrations courtesy the Bridgeman Art Library.

Page 16: Grant of Arms to New East India Company, 1698. Guildhall Library, City of London.

Page 21: *Scene in the Bohea Mountains, on Marco Polo's Route between Jiangsu and Fukien*, engraving from *The Book of Ser Marco Polo*, ed. Yule, published 1903. Private collection.

Page 22: English School, *The Tea Party*. Oil on canvas. Private collection.

Page 24: *British Stamps for America, 1765*. Lithograph. Published in *Harper's Magazine* in 1876. Private collection/Peter Newark Pictures.

Page 27: American School (18th century), *Samuel Adams*, c. 1770–72. Oil on canvas. Photo © Collection of the New-York Historical Society.

Page 44: American School (19th century), *The Dartmouth in Boston Harbour*. Lithograph. Private collection/Peter Newark American Pictures.

Page 52: Boston Tea Party tea leaves in a glass bottle, collected by T. M. Harris, Dorchester Neck, December 1773. Photo © Massachusetts Historical Society, Boston.

Page 54: American School (18th century), *Tea Destroyed by Indians*, American broadside praising "Ye Glorious sons of Freedom" for raiding the British tea ships, 1773. Lithograph. Private collection/Peter Newark American Pictures.

Page 63: American School (18th century), *The Bostonians Paying the Exciseman, or Tarring and Feathering*. Engraving. American Antiquarian Society, Worcester, Massachusetts.

Page 67: "The Medley of Goods" imported from foreign lands advertised by a New York merchant, 1769. Lithograph. Private collection/Peter Newark American Pictures.

Page 75: Reverend Samuel Manning, *County Court House, or Independence Hall, Philadelphia, Pennsylvania*, c. 1880. Lithograph. Private collection/Ken Welsh.

Page 96: *Plan of New York in 1729*. Lithograph. Private collection/Peter Newark American Pictures.

Page 101: Matthew Pratt (1734–1805), *Cadwallader Colden*, Oil on canvas. Photo © Collection of the New-York Historical Society.

Page 108: American School, after a painting by Howard Pyle, *On the River Front of New York City (South Street on the East River in the 18th century)*. Lithograph. Private Collection/Peter Newark American Pictures.

Page 111: Proclamation informing the public of how a British tea ship was prevented from landing cargo at New York, April 19, 1774. Lithograph. Private Collection/ Peter Newark American Pictures/ The Bridgeman Art Library

Page 124: American School (18th century), *James Nicholson*, c. 1795. Oil on canvas. Photo © Collection of the New-York Historical Society.

Page 132: English School (19th century), *John Adams*, from "Gallery of Historical Portraits," published c. 1880. Lithograph. Private collection/Ken Welsh.

Page 135: Fishermen drying cod in New England, from a 17th-century woodcut. Color lithograph. Private collection/Peter Newark American Pictures.

Page 167: Philip Dawe (d. 1832), *Patriotic Ladies of Edenton, South Carolina, Sign a Pledge "Not to drink any more tea, nor wear any more British cloth."* Lithograph. Private collection/Peter Newark Pictures.

Acknowledgments

I'd like to thank my editor, Jason Rekulak, whose humor and insights have helped me illuminate, once again, a little-explored area of American history. Also thanks to Doogie Horner, for his handsome book design, and Mary Ellen Wilson, for her attentive copyediting.

I also wish to thank my researcher, Michael Gately, who dug into some really dusty corners to come up with interesting and unexpected tea-party stories.

Books that were especially helpful include Benjamin L. Carp's wonderful *Defiance of the Patriots: The Boston Tea Party and the Making of America*; T. H. Breen's eye-opening *The Marketplace of the Revolution: How Consumer Politics Shaped American Independence*; and both volumes of William H. Uker's classic *All About Tea*. Special thanks to Adam Goodheart for his article "Tea and Fantasy," in the autumn 2005 issue of *The American Scholar*, which delves deeply and entertainingly into the mystery of the Chestertown Tea Party.

Last but not least, my love to Dede and Carson, both stellar tea-sots.